ORTHO'S All Abo

D0128841

Perennials

Written by Ann Lovejoy and Jan Riggenbach

Meredith® Books
Des Moines, Iowa

Ortho® Books
An imprint of Meredith® Books

Ortho's All About Perennials
Editor: Michael McKinley
Art Director: Tom Wegner
Copy Chief: Catherine Hamrick
Copy and Production Editor: Terri Fredrickson
Contributing Editors: James A. Baggett,
   Leona Holdsworth Openshaw
Contributing Writer: Martin Miller
Technical Consultant: Dr. Allan M. Armitage
Contributing Copy Editor: Chardel Gibson Blaine
Technical Research Assistant: Carolyn S. Magnani
Technical Proofreader: Mary Pas
Contributing Proofreaders: Kathy Eastman, JoEllyn Witke
Contributing Illustrators: Mike Eagleton, Pam Wattenmaker
Contributing Map Illustrator: Jana Fothergill
Contributing Prop/Photo Stylists: Mary E. Klingaman,
   Diane Munkel, Pamela K. Peirce
Indexer: Donald Glassman
Electronic Production Coordinator: Paula Forest
Editorial and Design Assistants: Kathleen Stevens,
   Karen Schirm
Production Director: Douglas M. Johnston
Production Manager: Pam Kvitne
Assistant Prepress Manager: Marjorie J. Schenkelberg

Additional Editorial Contributions from
   Art Rep Services
Director: Chip Nadeau
Designers: Teresa Marone, Laura Rades

Meredith® Books
Editor in Chief: James D. Blume
Design Director: Matt Strelecki
Managing Editor: Gregory H. Kayko
Executive Ortho Editor: Benjamin W. Allen

Director, Sales & Marketing, Retail: Michael A. Peterson
Director, Sales & Marketing, Special Markets:
   Rita McMullen
Director, Sales & Marketing, Home & Garden Center
   Channel: Ray Wolf
Director, Operations: George A. Susral

Vice President, General Manager: Jamie L. Martin

Meredith Publishing Group
President, Publishing Group: Christopher M. Little
Vice President, Consumer Marketing & Development:
   Hal Oringer

Meredith Corporation
Chairman and Chief Executive Officer: William T. Kerr
Chairman of the Executive Committee: E.T. Meredith III

On the cover: Bearded iris with lupine. Photograph by Allan Mandell.

All of us at Ortho® Books are dedicated to providing you with the information and ideas you need to enhance your home and garden. We welcome your comments and suggestions about this book. Write to us at:
   Meredith Corporation
   Ortho Books
   1716 Locust St.
   Des Moines, IA 50309–3023

Thanks to
 Sue Carver, Melissa George, Colleen Johnson, Callie McRoskey, Aimee Reiman, Mary Irene Swartz, and Sloat Garden Center of San Francisco, California

Photographers
(Photographers credited may retain copyright ©
   to the listed photographs.)
L= Left, R= Right, C= Center, B= Bottom, T= Top
David Cavagnaro: 17BR, 64BC, 64BR, 77T, 79C, 82C, 82B, 85CL, 89B; Walter Chandoha: 80TL, 80C; R. Todd Davis: 48C, 68 Row2-2, 71CCT, 71CR, 75 BL, 90B; Alan L. Detrick: 35TL, 68 Row 1-1, 79CR Alan & Linda Detrick: 25TL, 35TR, 68 Row 2-1, 68BL; Catriona Tudor Erler: 19TL; Derek Fell: 18T, 24TL, 25RCB, 49B, 62T, 63TC, 63TRBR, 63C, 64T, 65B, 67T, 77CBR, 84BL; Charles Marden Fitch: 56T, 68 Row 2-4, 79TC; John Glover: 24TR, 26TL, 26TC, 73B, 78BR inset, 86TL; David Goldberg: 35BR & inset, 39 all, 40, 41T, 43B all; Harry Haralambou: 57B, 76T; Jessie M. Harris: 52B, 54T, 68 Row 1-4, 68 Row 2-3, 68BC, 71BC, 71BR, 91BL; Lynne Harrison: 64C, 66C, 70TL; Jerry Harpur: 5C, 14, 27BL, 46, 58T, 75C, 76C; Marcus Harpur: 25RTC; Glenn Jahnke: 5BL, 5BC; Bill Johnson: 52TL, 70C, 79TR Mark Kane: 69C, 77BR, 91TL; Andrew Lawson: 8TL, 9TL, 11, 15, 18C, 24BL, 26LCT, 26BR, 27TR, 27BR, 48B, 52C, 56C, 57CR, 63B, 66B, 67B inset, 68 Row 1-2, 73T, 79BL, 85TL, 91TR; Erich Lessing/Art; Resource, NY: 30T; Janet Loughrey: 70BL; Allan Mandell: 4BR, 7TR, 7BL, 8TR, 8BR, 16T, 16B, 17T, 17BL, 22C, 22BR, 23T, 23C, 26TR, 27TL, 28 all, 29 all, 30BR, 31, 36, 59C, 66TL, 68BR; Charles Mann: 50T, 55T, 59BR, 63TRBL, 65C, 81CL, 81B, 83T; Bryan McCay: 37CL, 37C, 37CR, 38TR, 38BR; David McDonald/PhotoGarden: 19TR, 24B inset, 30BC, 47C, 59T, 63TRT, 66TC, 67B, 75T, 84TR, 87BR, 88BL; Michael McKinley: 4BL, 6TL, 6TR, 6BR, 7TL, 9BL, 10TR, 19B, 34, 47T, 47B, 51T, 51C, 53C, 53B, 55C, 56B, 57T, 62B, 69B, 70CR, 70BC, 74C, 74BL, 74BR, 81T, 84TL, 84BR, 86CL, 86BL, 87CR, 88T; Clive Nichols: 10TL (The Old Rectory, Burghfield, Berkshire), 62C, 87T (Wendy Lauderdale); Arthur N. Orans/Horticultural Photography: 54C; Maggie Oster: 25TR, 30BL, 49C, 50C, 50B, 57CL, 60B, 68 Row 1-3, 72 all, 74T, 78CL, 78BC, 79BC, 82T, 85CR, 89C, 90C; Jerry Pavia: 18B, 25BL, 32 all, 33 all, 48T, 61B, 67C, 69T, 71CCB, 83C, 85B, 88C, 91BR; Graham Rice/New Leaf Images: 51B, 53T; Cheryl R. Richter: 55BR; Susan A. Roth: 19C, 42 all, 49TL, 49TR, 52TC, 54B, 55BC, 58C, 60T, 60C, 61T, 61C, 70TC, 70TR, 75BR, 76B, 77CTR, 77CBL, 78TL, 78BL, 79TL, 81CR, 83B, 85TR, 86TR, 87CL, 87BL, 90T, 91CL; Richard Shiell: 59BL, 65T; Sheri Sparks: 5CR, 5BR; Albert; Squillace/Positive Images: 26BL, 89T; Studio Central: 22BL, 43T all; Michael S. Thompson: 25BR, 26LCB, 58B, 64BL, 71TC, 71TR, 73C, 80TR, 80B, 84CR, 88BR, 91CR; Mark Turner: 84CL; Patricia Wadecki: 5CL; Marilyn Warford/Horticultural Photography: 79CL; Kay Wheeler 9TR, 79BR; judywhite/New Leaf Images: 10BR, 41B

Note to the Readers: Due to differing conditions, tools, and individual skills, Meredith Corporation assumes no responsibility for any damages, injuries suffered, or losses incurred as a result of following the information published in this book. Before beginning any project, review the instructions carefully, and if any doubts or questions remain, consult local experts or authorities. Because codes and regulations vary greatly, you always should check with authorities to ensure that your project complies with all applicable local codes and regulations. Always read and observe all of the safety precautions provided by manufacturers of any tools, equipment, or supplies, and follow all accepted safety procedures.

P4 7 20

A PROGRESSION OF PERENNIALS

GARDEN STARS

Across America, gardeners are discovering the ease, versatility, and colorful seasonal drama of perennials. Bold masses of sedum, fountain grass, and Joe-Pye weed bring late-summer color to a Maryland new American garden (left), while a cottage garden in Seattle pairs neighborly delphinium and yarrow (right).

If trees, shrubs, and vines are the workhorses of a garden, then perennials are the stars. A well-chosen succession of perennials will supply gardens anywhere with months of colorful, ever-changing drama.

Unlike annual flowers, which bloom, set seed, and die in a single growing season, perennials are more permanent plants. Some are short-lived, surviving only two or three growing seasons. But most are long-lived, thriving for decades. Some are evergreen. Many, however, are herbaceous, which means that their foliage goes dormant and dies down to the ground (usually in fall), but reappears the next spring. Selected for overlapping bloom, perennials can create waves of color from early spring until the first frost.

While most perennials bloom for shorter periods than annuals (a few all-stars bloom for two months or more), many boast handsome foliage that creates a strong and lasting contribution to the garden picture. Some perennials have summer-long leaves as colorful as any flower. And many can be as structural as any shrub or small tree.

Because they mature faster than trees or shrubs, perennials are an excellent way to achieve quick effect in the landscape—often by the second season after planting. Grown in beds and borders, perennial flowers, ferns, and grasses can be massed in colorful drifts that emphasize potent contrasts of leaf size, texture, and color. In mixed borders—which may contain trees, shrubs, and vines, as well as bulbs and annuals—perennials soften the stiffness of evergreens, mask dying bulb foliage, and fill in empty bays between shrubs with color. Perennials can burst out of the border as well, spilling from pots and containers at patio or entryway, pouring across the ground in richly textured carpets, weaving into dainty or bold tapestries beneath trees.

This book is designed to help you grow perennials effectively in the home landscape. On the following pages we will explore the plants and flowers that each season brings, the form and structure they lend to the garden border, as well as how to combine and extend their season of interest. And, of course, we will arm you with all the basics you'll need to find and successfully grow just the right plants for your own garden.

PERENNIALS IN THE LANDSCAPE

Traditional, formal English perennial borders have inspired many American gardeners. But they are often labor intensive, and dependent on the mild, moist English climate seldom found in this country. Cottage gardens, however, with their loose design and cheerful profusion of annuals and perennials, make an excellent model, providing that plants adapted to this country are used.

Garden designers on this side of the Atlantic have combined the cottage-garden concept with the American spirit of adventure and created what some call "the new American garden." While loose and naturalistic in effect, redolent of meadows and woodlands, the hallmark of the new American garden is the arrangement of sturdy, easy-care perennials in bold, painterly strokes across the ground, with large beds of the same kind of plant often numbering in the hundreds. Groups of taller perennials (especially dramatic grasses), shrubs, and trees are then used to lift this colorful groundplane into vertical, sculptural relief, as well as to "knit" together the boundary between two masses of low plants.

Good perennial partnerships involve more than just esthetics. As in any relationship, the best companions have compatible cultural needs and habits, or manner of growth. Perennial partners should complement each other in color, form, size, texture, and period of bloom. Well-chosen, well-paired, and well-placed plants will be happy, healthy ones. The best partners are cooperators, adaptive plants that share their space and resources well.

HOW TO SEQUENCE SEASONS

To create a sequence of color effects, we need to create combinations that carry a theme throughout the seasons.

Beautiful, long-flowering natural models offer us the means and methods to achieve this effect. Consider the tallgrass prairie, the mountain meadow, or the woodland. Each displays a specific tapestry of interwoven perennials, annuals, grasses, and bulbs growing almost on top of one another. In the garden we call this "sandwich planting." Cut out a cross section of prairie sod and you'll see roots layered like a club sandwich.

Don't think of garden soil in terms of square feet. Think cubically, and the options increase dramatically. The same cubic foot of earth can house five or six (or even more) types of compatible plants that will perform in one wave after the other. As the low-growing, early bloomers go dormant, larger summer stars arise to take their place. These eventually give way to the towering flowers of fall, many of which persist as striking, lovely skeletons well into the winter. The result is a yearly drama of ever-changing beauty.

For thousands of years the stretch of virgin prairie shown below has performed a seasonal drama of astonishing richness and diversity—one botanist counted 2,600 plants to the square meter! These six images reflect different seasons on the same piece of land.

MAY: A carpet of shooting star, bird's-foot violet, and orange puccoon

JUNE: Knee-high purple coneflower and an early goldenrod

JULY: Black-eyed Susan and grasses lift the prairie above the knees.

AUGUST: Waist-high spiky blazing star stretches to the prairie's horizon.

SEPTEMBER: Joe-Pye weed and sunflowers raise the prairie overhead.

DECEMBER: Grasses glisten under a coating of ice on the snowy prairie.

A generous planting of creeping phlox provides a blanket of color in an "alpine meadow" (left). Purple blossoms of pasque flower raise their heads in a detail of the same meadow (right).

SPRING BLOOMERS

FOR SUN

Cushion spurge
  (*Euphorbia
  polychroma*)
Globe flower (*Trollius
  × cultorum*)
Heartleaf bergenia
  (*Bergenia cordifolia*)
Leopard's bane
  (*Doronicum
  caucasicum*)
Marsh marigold (*Caltha
  palustris*)
Rock cress
  (*Aurinia saxatilis*)

FOR SHADE

Bishop's hat
  (*Epimedium
  grandiflorum*)
Bleeding heart
  (*Dicentra
  spectabilis*)
Blue corydalis
  (*Corydalis flexuosa*)
Columbine (*Aquilegia*)
Lenten rose
  (*Helleborus
  orientalis*)
Lungwort (*Pulmonaria
  officinalis*)
Primrose
  (*Primula*)
Sweet violet
  (*Viola odorata*)
Wood anemone
  (*Anemone nemerosa*)

FIRST FLOWERS

In early spring, garden beds and borders green up fast. Sleepy perennials stretch skyward as temperatures rise. Some of them, the hardiest, begin to bloom as the snow melts. Others leaf out first, and then their fresh foliage is quickly followed by plump buds and cheerful flowers.

To find early bloomers suited to your region and climate, spend some time at a local nursery, garden center, or botanical garden. Mail-order and on-line catalogs will increase choices, as will plant swaps sponsored by your local plant societies. If you live in a mild climate, your choices will be plentiful. Harsh winters may alter that selection. Regardless of where you live, the hunt for early-blooming flowers presents an exciting challenge that can extend the garden year.

HOW TO COMBINE EARLY BLOOMS FOR IMPACT

To develop vivid early color, arrange these first-flowering plants in clusters, keeping together those whose needs and colors are similar. Instead of dotting them in sparse patches around the garden, group them in sufficient quantities to make an impact.

Take a cue from nature; your garden plantings can be sandwiched literally into the same piece of ground, so that your first flowers are followed by second and third waves

in the same location. Spring flowers don't have to simply appear on trees and shrubs or bulbs. Look to nature and you'll find plenty of perennial early risers, such as sweet violet (*Viola*) and fringed bleeding heart (*Dicentra*). Dozens of other native species flower in spring, as do their hybrid cousins. Consider tucking clumps of early perennials between larger and later-rising plants; they will bloom early and remain as a ground cover.

Besides the purplish green lenten rose (*Helleborus orientalis*), the anemone family is a terrific source for early color: fuzzy-budded pasque flower (*Pulsatilla vulgaris*) is excellent for well-drained, sunny sites. Lacy-leaved wood anemone (*Anemone nemorosa*) naturalizes in blankets of white in shady locations. Native to the southeastern United States, blue star (*Amsonia tabernaemontana*) retains its attractive, willowlike foliage long after its clusters of blue flowers open in spring. And after the spring blooms of columbine (*Aquilegia*) have faded, the textured foliage continues to provide interest (and hide dying bulb foliage) throughout the summer.

Shady gardens are ideal for woodland flowers, many of which bloom early, then go dormant as summer heat builds. To hide the gaps they leave behind, mingle them with plants whose foliage comes into their own later.

Planted in the border, poppies and peonies share summer's colorful stage (left). A summer composition of red roses surrounded by foxglove, iris, and allium (right) makes a dramatic statement.

EARLY-SUMMER COLOR

By early summer, many gardens are fragrant with roses, lilies, and honeysuckle, but apart from peonies (*Paeonia*), foxglove (*Digitalis*), and coral bells (*Heuchera*), perennials appear in short supply. Some gardeners select flowers that all bloom at approximately the same time for a garden filled with color. This creates a spectacular, but brief, display. Unfortunately, it also means there is little or no perennial bloom for the rest of the season.

Gardeners who prefer a longer duration of early summer color, plant for a continuous succession of bloom, with new flowers coming as spring flowers fade past bloom. This may seem to dilute the impact of the overall color scheme, but it actually reveals more of the complete character of the plants. In general, even when the garden is planned and planted with succession in mind, there are still three or four peak periods during the season, interspersed with periods of quiet green relief.

With the variations in blossoming times and the duration of bloom, the possibilities for the early summer perennial garden are immense. Sequencers—plants that remain effective throughout the seasons—help bridge the gap between these peak periods. Meadow rue (*Thalictrum*), for example, makes a super sequencer; its airy scrim adds a sense of mystery to the small garden and screens over sweeps of browning bulb foliage. Ornamental grasses, mounded spirea shrubs, woolly lamb's-ears (*Stachys byzantina*), and *Verbena bonariensis* are all excellent sequencers.

HOW TO MAKE IT LAST

Many early-summer perennials can also provide you with decorative effects over additional seasons. In early summer, false indigo (*Baptisia australis*)—with its sweet pealike flowers in blue or white—doubles as a splendid foliage plant. Its lustrous blue-gray foliage partners pleasantly with long-fingered peonies and the slender wands of peach-leaf bellflower (*Campanula persicifolia*). Indigo foliage remains sturdy into winter and provides a handsome backdrop for late bloomers. In shady sites, try clumps of foxglove and aster, which are long-blooming. Bellflower, too, lasts longer than a single season. And if spent blooms are cut back, they'll likely send up a fresh flush of flowers.

Bright orange blossoms of naturalized candelabra primroses add interest to a shady woodland mixed border (above).

EARLY SUMMER BLOOMERS

FOR SUN
Bellflower (*Campanula*)
Butterfly weed (*Asclepias tuberosa*)
Common peony (*Paeonia officinalis*)
Delphinium (*Delphinium* × *elatum*)
Dwarf crested iris (*Iris cristata*)
Oriental poppy (*Papaver*)
Pink (*Dianthus*)
Siberian iris (*Iris siberica*)
Threadleaf coreopsis (*Coreopsis verticillata*)
Variegated iris (*Iris pallida* 'Variegata')

FOR SHADE
Coral bells (*Heuchera*)
Foxglove (*Digitalis purpurea*)
Hardy geranium (*Geranium macrorrhizum*)
Lady's mantle (*Alchemilla mollis*)
Chinese rhubarb (*Rheum palmatum*)
Woodland phlox (*Phlox divaricata*)

A traditional summer border designed by Christopher Lloyd layers colors (left). Wands of vibrant red Crocosmia *'Lucifer' creates seasonal impact (right).*

HIGH-SUMMER PERENNIALS

FOR SUN
Blazing star (*Liatris spicata*)
Daylily (*Hemerocallis*)
Hollyhock mallow (*Malva alcea*)
Joe-Pye weed (*Eupatorium purpureum*)
Queen-of-the-prairie (*Filipendula rubra*)
Red valerian (*Centranthus ruber*)
Sea holly (*Eryngium amethystinum*)
Tree mallow (*Lavatera thuringiaca*)
Yarrow (*Achillea*)

FOR SHADE
Astilbe (*Astilbe arendsii*)
Goatsbeard (*Aruncus dioicus*)
Hosta (*Hosta*)
Japanese painted fern (*Athyrium nipponicum*)
Lady fern (*Athyrium filix-femina*)
Maidenhair fern (*Adiantum pedatum*)

HIGH-SUMMER DISPLAY

High summer is show time in the garden: To create that dazzling array of nonstop fireworks, pay attention to the average bloom time of your favorite perennials. Once you know how they behave in your own backyard, you can concoct potent combinations, interweaving flowers and foliage. When one plant takes a breather, another can step in and take its place. Track performance in a garden journal or notebook and use the bloom season chart on pages 12 and 13 to help you.

HOW TO GROW A VARIETY SHOW

The best way to enjoy an unbroken sequence of bloom is to develop a full palette of perennial color. (It helps to shop all year round, choosing seasonal bests.) Variety ensures that despite quirky weather, disease, or nuisance animals, something will succeed. Begin with garden workhorses, plants with staying power in almost any situation. Yarrow (*Achillea*), sedum, daylily (*Hemerocallis*), and similar tireless plants come in a range of sizes and colors.

Don't stop with color. Group your choices by shape and texture as well. Many perennials are basically mound-shaped and need contrasts to keep their own identity. Choose yucca, Chinese rhubarb (*Rheum palmatum*), mullein (*Verbascum*), sea holly (*Eryngium*), and fountain grass (*Pennisetum*).

SUN OR SHADE?

Sunny gardens can host a tremendous number of summer bloomers. Among them are many native flowers that adapt effortlessly to the home landscape, growing larger and blooming longer than they do in the wild. Purple coneflower (*Echinacea purpurea*) and blanket flower (*Gaillardia*), black-eyed Susan (*Rudbeckia*) and beard-tongue (*Penstemon*) all provide multiple possibilities throughout the summer season.

Shady woodland gardens are often quite dry by midsummer. Where water is an issue, select drought-tolerant plants. If it's damp shade you have, dozens of perennials suit it to a "T," from spiky ligularia to bold rodgersia. Damp or dry, shade gardens can hold marvelous tapestries of foliage perennials such as hosta and lungwort (*Pulmonaria*). For contrast, mix in rounded and ruffled coral bells (*Heuchera*), lacy ferns, and fine-textured astilbes.

Variegated hosta, Japanese painted fern, and foam flower blanket a shady woodland garden.

A spectacular late-summer border filled with aster, black-eyed Susan, and tassels of goldenrod (left). White, yellow, and orange chrysanthemums and dried grasses enliven the fall landscape (right).

LATE BLOOMERS

As late summer melts into autumn, warm days and cool nights waken the hidden flames of foliage. Blue star (*Amsonia taberaemontana*) and balloon flower (*Platycodon*) turn to fiery gold. Variegated obedient plant (*Physostegia*) reblooms above foliage streaked with raspberry and cream.

HOW TO EXTEND AUTUMN

In order to have a good autumnal show, you must dedicate significant garden space to some of these late bloomers. It need not mean a summer sacrifice: If 10 to 20 percent of your plants offer strong fall flower or foliage color, they will carry the season. Keep in mind, many late performers are large plants with plenty of character. They are standouts. What's more, you can place them behind rebloomers, (yarrow, blanket flower, and daylily), whose contribution will now be amplified by their dramatic neighbors.

A shady slate pathway is flanked by colorful foliage plants arranged for textural interest.

To maximize your autumn display, group late bloomers in clusters and sweeps, and give them supportive companions (such as long-season foliage plants and additional reliable rebloomers), so the fall performers do not appear forlorn or as an afterthought in the home landscape. And select fall flowers that can pull their weight over several seasons, such as sedum, black-eyed Susan (*Rudbeckia fulgida*), and the structurally fascinating *Aster lateriflorus* var. *horizontalis*.

SUCCESS WITH NATIVES

Native plants excel in the autumn landscape. The golden tassels of goldenrod (*Solidago*) burn against the sky, and asters haze the garden with smoky blue and purple. Native switch grasses (*Panicum virgatum*) 'Heavy Metal' and 'Cloud Nine' shimmer like spun gold. Indeed, a host of other grasses bring glitter and gleam to fall gardens, from maiden grass (*Miscanthus sinensis*) such as 'Morning Light' or zebra-striped 'Stricta' to dwarfs such as Mexican feather grass (*Stipa tenuissima*) and Japanese blood grass (*Imperata cylindrica* 'Red Baron').

In shady gardens, bugbane (*Cimicifuga racemosa*) and the white flowers of *Hosta plantaginea* scent the air. Rosy or creamy, Japanese anemone blooms long and hard in dappled light. Arching wands of toad lily (*Tricyrtis hirta*) are studded with tiny flowers. And when the foliage tapestry is turning golden, there are evergreen ferns and Lenten roses to carry on the spectacle throughout winter.

LATE PERFORMERS

FOR SUN
Blue star
  (*Amsonia tabernaemontana*)
Boltonia
  (*Boltonia asteroides*)
Goldenrod
  (*Solidago*)
Hardy aster
  (*Aster*)
Helen's flower
  (*Helenium autumnale*)
Plumbago
  (*Ceratostigma plumbaginoides*)
Stonecrop
  (*Sedum spectabile*)
FOR SHADE
Bugbane
  (*Cimicifuga racemosa*)
Cardinal flower
  (*Lobelia cardinalis*)
Japanese anemone
  (*Anemone × hybrida*)
Monkshood
  (*Aconitum*)
Toad lily
  (*Tricyrtis hirta*)

Deadheads catch the frost in a formal border (left). Grasses and black-eyed Susans last through winter (right).

COLD-WINTER INTEREST

FOR SUN

Black-eyed Susan
  (*Rudbeckia fulgida*)
False indigo
  (*Baptisia australis*)
Giant feather grass
  (*Stipa gigantea*)
Globe thistle (*Echinops
  bannaticus*)
Joe-Pye weed
  (*Eupatorium
  purpureum*)
Mullein
  (*Verbascum chaixii*)
Pinks
  (*Dianthus*)
Sea holly
  (*Eryngium
  amthystinum*)
Stonecrop
  (*Sedum spectabile*)
Yucca
  (*Yucca filamentosa*)

FOR SHADE

Barrenwort
  (*Epimedium* ×
  rubrum)
Golden grass
  (*Hakonechloa macra*)

CONSIDER THE GARDEN IN WINTER

Winter in the garden does not need to be a down time. Its subtle beauty lies in line and form. Cold winter gardens can hold eye-catching shapes and textures. When sturdy, structural perennials are left to stand through wind, snow, and ice, the resulting shapes can work the same magic which transforms a meadow from stubble to sculpture.

HOW TO MAKE A CHEERFUL SPLASH

Where mild winters are the rule (zones 7, 8, and 9), the garden possibilities become far more plentiful. Evergreen perennials come into their own when earlier blooming, brasher competition retreats. Grouped and given the support of compact border shrubs (evergreen herbs, rhododendrons, and dwarf conifers), even the least showy winter flowers can make a cheerful splash.

Winter is an excellent time to study the flow and follow-through of garden color. Journal notes will help you rule out the less suitable and rearrange better performers for winter appeal. Through selection and editing, you can develop your own winter perennial palette to enliven this underappreciated season. By leaving seed heads in place, you'll also get a bonus of birds visiting the winter garden with moving color.

As you expand your palette with off-season performers, you may need to make room by cutting back on spring- and summer-blooming flowers. Start by replacing plants that no longer thrill you, supplanting them with late bloomers. Take advantage of the season to study specialty catalogs for plants to try. Before long, the flow of overlapping color will extend throughout the seasons.

Woodland winters are wonderfully quiet. Grasses whisper in the breeze, their hollow stems rustling softly. Blanketing snow emphasizes the graceful silhouettes of purple coneflower (*Echinacea purpurea*), with stems the color of burnt earth. Brown and burnished, the skeletons of Joe-Pye weed (*Eupatorium purpureum*) cast shadows on the snow, joined by native goldenrod (*Solidago*).

The pale green flowers and dark green foliage of Lenten rose look lovely in snow.

HOW TO TRACK THE SEQUENCE OF THE SEASONS

If color themes are to change with the seasons, timing becomes critical. The chart that follows on pages 12 and 13 is a good way to begin, but any book can offer only a general idea of how plants perform. What happens in your garden is specific to your region and climate. The best way to track performance is by keeping regular records in a garden journal. You don't need to make voluminous notes, and you don't have to write in it every day.

■ Record what you've planted, where, along with rainfall and temperature.

■ Note what's in bloom so you can have an idea of the general flow of each season through the garden year.

■ Take snapshots to remember where and when plants bloomed. Study them to find new combinations.

■ Keep a calendar in the garage or garden shed indicating your spray and fertilizer schedules from year to year.

■ Jot down the beginning and ending dates of all perennials each year. Patterns will emerge, and soon you'll be better able to combine plant selections in order to extend the season of interest.

MILD-WINTER INTEREST

FOR SUN
Anise hyssop
   (*Agastache foeniculum*)
Feather reed grass
   (*Calamagrostis × acutiflora*)
Maiden grass
   (*Miscanthus sinensis*)
New Zealand flax
   (*Phormium tenax*)
Pampas grass
   (*Cortaderia selloana*)
Switch grass
   (*Panicum virgatum*)
Twinspur
   (*Diascia barberae*)
FOR SHADE
Bergenia
   (*Bergenia cordifolia*)
Stokes' aster
   (*Stokesia laevis*)
Variegated Japanese sedge
   (*Carex morrowii 'Variegata'*)

Spring's succession: Pastel tulips and daffodils anchor this early mixed border that abuts a stone house. The flowers are underplanted with forget-me-nots at the front of the border to create a pleasing transition to the lawn.

Summer's succession: The same mixed border a few weeks later boasts a vivid new palette that includes iris, hardy geranium, lady's mantle, and balloon flower, which mask passing bulb foliage.

Autumn's succession: As summer recedes, so do its star performers. Strong bursts of rust and yellow foliage fill the same mixed border—filled in with ornamental kale and nasturtium—with harvest colors.

BLOOM SEASON CHART

Use this chart to help you plan overlapping seasons of bloom for color all year. Because perennials are listed in order of bloom, you can easily see at a glance which bloom together, which bloom in succession, and which bloom for extra long times. Remember that any bloom chart will only be a rough guide, as bloom seasons can differ according to the region, the weather, microclimates, and cultivars. Blue bars represent bloom seasons; orange bars represent fall foliage and fruit effects.

Plant Name	Spr. E	Spr. M	Spr. L	Sum. E	Sum. M	Sum. L	Fall E	Fall M	Fall L	Win. E	Win. M	Win. L
Basket-of-gold (Aurinia saxatilis)	■	■										
Bergenia (Bergenia cordifolia)	■	■	■				▓	▓	▓			
Marsh marigold (Caltha palustris)	■	■										
Red barrenwort (Epimedium × rubrum)	■	■						▓				
Cushion spurge (Euphorbia polychroma)	■	■										
Mediterranean spurge (Euphorbia characias)	■	■										
Lenten rose (Helleborus orientalis)	■	■										
Creeping phlox (Phlox subulata)	■											
Bethlehem sage (Pulmonaria saccharata)	■	■										
Sweet violet (Viola odorata)		■										
Bleeding heart (Dicentra spectabilis)		■										
Luxuriant bleeding heart (Dicentra 'Luxuriant')		■	■	■	■							
Myrtle spurge (Euphorbia myrsinites)	■	■					▓	▓				
English primrose (Primula vulgaris)		■										
Columbine (Aquilegia)		■	■									
False indigo (Baptisia australis)	■	■	■				▓	▓	▓			
Dwarf crested iris (Iris cristata)		■										
Cheddar pink (Dianthus gratianopolitanus)			■									
Woodland phlox (Phlox divaricata)		■	■									
Allegheny foam flower (Tiarella cordifolia)		■	■	■								
Lady's mantle (Alchemilla mollis)			■	■								
Blue star (Amsonia tabernaemontana)			■				▓	▓				
Astilbe (Astilbe × arendsii)			■	■			▓	▓	▓			
Masterwort (Astrantia major)			■	■								
Yellow corydalis (Corydalis lutea)			■	■	■	■						
Japanese primrose (Primula japonica)				■	■							
Peach-leaf bellflower (Campanula persicifolia)				■	■							
Red valerian (Centranthus ruber)				■	■	■						
Twinspur (Diascia barberae)				■	■	■	▓	▓				
Foxglove (Digitalis purpurea)				■	■							
Bloody cranesbill (Geranium sanguineum)				■	■		▓	▓				
Johnson's Blue hardy geranium (Geranium himalayense × 'Johnson's Blue')				■	■							
Geum (Geum)				■								

Plant Name	Spr. E	Spr. M	Spr. L	Sum. E	Sum. M	Sum. L	Fall E	Fall M	Fall L	Win. E	Win. M	Win. L
Creeping baby's breath (Gypsophila repens)				■	■	■						
Stella de Oro daylily (Hemerocallis 'Stella de Oro')				■	■	■						
Coral bells (Heuchera hybrids)				■	■							
Bearded iris, early season (Iris hybrids)				■								
Siberian iris (Iris sibirica)				■			▓	▓				
Lupine (Lupinus 'Russell Hybrid')				■	■							
Catmint (Nepeta × faassenii)				■	■	■						
Peony (Paeonia hybrids)				■								
Oriental poppy (Papaver orientale)				■	■							
Beard-tongue (Penstemon)				■	■							
Lamb's-ear (Stachys byzantina)				■	■							
Columbine meadow rue (Thalictrum aquilegiifolium)				■	■							
Variegated Solomon's seal (Polygonatum odoratum 'Variegatum')				■			▓	▓				
Coronation Gold yarrow (Achillea × 'Coronation Gold')				■	■	■	■			▓		
Hollyhock (Alcea rosea)				■	■							
Goatsbeard (Aruncus dioicus)				■								
Hybrid sage (Salvia × sylvestris)				■	■							
Delphinium (Delphinium × elatum)				■	■							
Butterfly weed (Asclepias tuberosa)				■	■		▓	▓				
Speedwell (Veronica hybrids)				■	■							
Kamtschatka stonecrop (Sedum kamtschaticum)				■	■							
Mullein (Verbascum chaixii)				■	■	■				▓		
Carpathian bellflower (Campanula carpatica)				■	■							
Common yarrow (Achillea millefolium)				■	■							
Maiden pink (Dianthus deltoides)				■	■							
Modern pink (Dianthus × allwoodii)				■	■							
Baby's breath (Gypsophila paniculata)					■		▓	▓				
Daylily (Hemerocallis)					■					▓		
Bearded iris, late season (Iris hybrids)					■							
Shasta daisy (Leucanthemum × superbum)					■	■						
Leopard's bane (Doronicum orientale)					■							
Threadleaf coreopsis (Coreopsis verticillata)					■	■						
Hardy geranium (Geranium psilostemon 'Bressingham Flair')					■		▓	▓				

Plant Name	Spr. E M L	Sum. E M L	Fall E M L	Win. E M L
Daylily, early season (*Hemerocallis*)				
Japanese iris (*Iris ensata*)				
Crimson pincushion (*Knautia macedonica*)				
Torch lily (*Kniphofia uvaria*)				
Tree mallow (*Lavatera thuringiaca*)				
Hollyhock mallow (*Malva alcea*)				
Golden lace (*Patrinia*)				
Chinese rhubarb (*Rheum palmatum*)				
Butterfly Blue pincushion flower (*Scabiosa columbaria* 'Butterfly Blue')				
Creeping verbena (*Verbena* hybrids)				
Sunny Border Blue speedwell (*Veronica* 'Sunny Border Blue')				
Feather reed grass (*Calamagrostis × acutiflora* 'Stricta')				
Tickseed (*Coreopsis grandiflora*)				
Blanket flower (*Gaillardia × grandiflora*)				
Frances Williams hosta (*Hosta sieboldiana* 'Frances Williams')				
Crocosmia (*Crocosmia* hybrids)				
Tufted hair grass (*Deschampsia caespitosa*)				
Globe thistle (*Echinops bannaticus*)				
Fleabane (*Erigeron* hybrids)				
Autumn Joy stonecrop (*Sedum/Hylotelephium* 'Autumn Joy'/ 'Herbstfreude')				
Yucca (*Yucca filamentosa*)				
Plumbago (*Ceratostigma plumbaginoides*)				
Queen-of-the-prairie (*Filipendula rubra*)				
Blue oat grass (*Helictotrichon sempervirens*)				
Purple moor grass (*Molinia caerulea* 'Variegata')				
Bee balm (*Monarda didyma*)				
Russian sage (*Perovskia atriplicifolia*)				
Rodgersia (*Rodgersia pinnata*)				
Stokes' aster (*Stokesia laevis*)				
Plume poppy (*Macleaya cordata*)				
Giant feather grass (*Stipa gigantea*)				
Monch Frikart's aster (*Aster x frikartii* 'Monch')				
Chinese astilbe (*Astilbe chinensis*)				
Bugbane (*Cimicifuga racemosa*)				

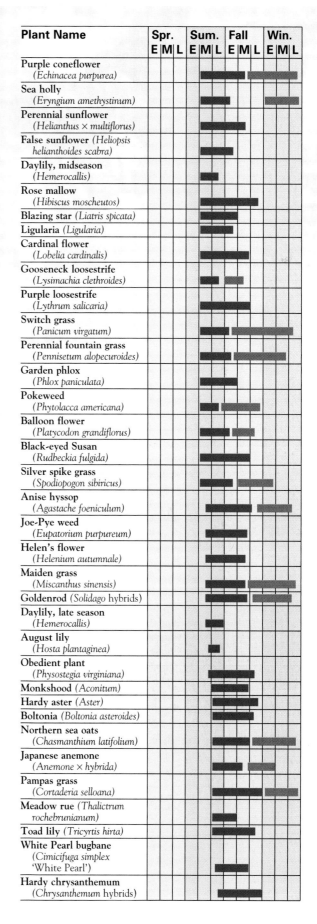

Plant Name	Spr. E M L	Sum. E M L	Fall E M L	Win. E M L
Purple coneflower (*Echinacea purpurea*)				
Sea holly (*Eryngium amethystinum*)				
Perennial sunflower (*Helianthus × multiflorus*)				
False sunflower (*Heliopsis helianthoides scabra*)				
Daylily, midseason (*Hemerocallis*)				
Rose mallow (*Hibiscus moscheutos*)				
Blazing star (*Liatris spicata*)				
Ligularia (*Ligularia*)				
Cardinal flower (*Lobelia cardinalis*)				
Gooseneck loosestrife (*Lysimachia clethroides*)				
Purple loosestrife (*Lythrum salicaria*)				
Switch grass (*Panicum virgatum*)				
Perennial fountain grass (*Pennisetum alopecuroides*)				
Garden phlox (*Phlox paniculata*)				
Pokeweed (*Phytolacca americana*)				
Balloon flower (*Platycodon grandiflorus*)				
Black-eyed Susan (*Rudbeckia fulgida*)				
Silver spike grass (*Spodiopogon sibiricus*)				
Anise hyssop (*Agastache foeniculum*)				
Joe-Pye weed (*Eupatorium purpureum*)				
Helen's flower (*Helenium autumnale*)				
Maiden grass (*Miscanthus sinensis*)				
Goldenrod (*Solidago* hybrids)				
Daylily, late season (*Hemerocallis*)				
August lily (*Hosta plantaginea*)				
Obedient plant (*Physostegia virginiana*)				
Monkshood (*Aconitum*)				
Hardy aster (*Aster*)				
Boltonia (*Boltonia asteroides*)				
Northern sea oats (*Chasmanthium latifolium*)				
Japanese anemone (*Anemone × hybrida*)				
Pampas grass (*Cortaderia selloana*)				
Meadow rue (*Thalictrum rochebrunianum*)				
Toad lily (*Tricyrtis hirta*)				
White Pearl bugbane (*Cimicifuga simplex* 'White Pearl')				
Hardy chrysanthemum (*Chrysanthemum* hybrids)				

FORM AND STRUCTURE IN THE GARDEN

A mixed border emphasizing the architectural structure and strong texture of perennials is designed in tiers that create a pleasing transition and composition.

To get the best performance from your garden, don't just pick plants with pretty colors. Remember texture, form, structure, and foliage. Flower colors are important, but it's the whole plant and where it will be placed that decides the complete picture. Keep in mind that the same plant that belongs at the back of a border (which is intended to be viewed only from one side) is the same plant that belongs in the center of a bed (which lacks a structural background and is viewed from all sides).

Don't forget those problem areas; open, exposed sites mean perennials must be drought and wind tolerant. Plants destined for seaside gardens must adapt to salty ocean spray. Woodlands may have permanently boggy spots or be bone dry in summer.

Regional and specialty nurseries are an invaluable source of information, ideas, and assistance. Many carry site-adaptive perennials for every need, from desert to bog.

HOW TO MAKE IT PERSONAL

Your garden should be personal: If you love a composition, then it's okay. But if you don't know where to start, consider these tips:

■ Play with your plants while they're in their pots. Arrange them in pleasing partnerships, creating contrasts of form and foliage.

■ Remember to consider the plant's ultimate size. Those inches-high asters in the spring may be five-foot giants by summer. Big plants shouldn't always be banished to the back. But unless they're airy in habit, they'll swamp the shorter plants you place behind them.

■ Plant compatibles. Partners in sun, dry soil, or moist shade must take equally to their conditions and placement or their relationship is doomed from the start. These plants must cooperate with one another.

■ If a plant ends up in the wrong place, it's usually pretty easy to move it. Don't be afraid to edit; the best gardens are often revised.

PLANTING IN LAYERS

Perennials are most often grown with plants of many kinds, usually arranged in tiers. Formal or naturalistic, layers give the garden a relaxed, abundant look, like a meadow or woodland. Whatever the style, the first tier serves as the carpet, where low-growing plants cover the ground and sprawlers can lace layers of the bed together. Next come intermediates, which make up the middle layer and provide a ladder between the front- and back-tier layers. The middle layer is like the forest understory, knit from compact shrubs and perennials.

In a large garden, each layer can be full size. In a smaller garden, you'll scale them down; shrubs will play the role of trees, and narrow, space-saving plants will substitute for plumper ones. But to start, begin at the back.

HOW TO DEFINE THE GARDEN

Third-tier plantings define the shape of the garden, so it's the place to begin. Third-tier plants create a canopy, treeline, or skyline of the tallest plants. They are often evergreen trees and shrubs which enclose the space like a hedge, rise to the highpoint in the center of an island, or form a backdrop in the border. The third tier establishes the garden line and can create a powerful silhouette. It's the third tier arrangement that will also set the tone, creating either a formal or casual feel. Ruffled, irregular layers help create an informal effect.

A straight line of any single plant, especially one with an architectural shape, suggests a crisp, clean edge. Formal gardens are most often geometrical and can be framed with third-tier plants whose lines are echoed by the others. They are edged and neatly shaped or sheared and are filled with massed plants or arranged in colorful or textured patterns.

Taller plants can occasionally be placed in front of shorter ones. This technique gives the beds a surprisingly different appearance when approached from different angles. It also creates a veil and an intriguing sense of mystery.

Many backdrop perennials spend spring and summer climbing skyward, reserving their bloom for late summer or autumn. When these plants offer flowers or foliage in the fall, then it's this framework that takes the stage itself. Grasses are natural candidates, with their bursts of color. Evergreen pampas grass (*Cortaderia selloana*) spreads great silken plumes. Some late-blooming goldenrods (*Solidago*) rise head high, while Joe-Pye weed (*Eupatorium*) looms taller still, producing a great mist of lavender-purple inflorescence.

But use care: Too-large plants can throw off the balance of scale, making everything else look dwarfed. The progression of perennials should be gradual, the topography intriguing. Backdrop plants should be dramatic ones that integrate themselves in the garden celebration with exciting form and color.

This formal border is an excellent example of planting in layers for an abundance of color, texture, and structure. Note how the front tier or front edge plantings soften the transition between bed and pathway.

MIDDLE AND LOW GROUND

First- and second-layer plants should merge with third-tier plantings, easing the eye groundward. Within these beds, more layers create an inner topography that plays up shape and texture. Relaxed interior arrangements create a fascinating flow of form as well as color. Consider these tiers once the bones of the garden have been determined.

Second-tier plantings create an intermediate layer between the first tier and the back border. In larger gardens, there may be two or three intermediate levels. In smaller beds, one layer will suffice. Intermediate layers link third-tier trees and taller plantings, creating a transition between the backdrop and the border's edge. In formal plantings, your intermediate layer will be uniform. Choose plants of consistent height and similar shape and arrange them in patterns to show the qualities that catch your eye. For an informal setting, you can plant a multiplicity of intermediate layers. You won't need to rank them so strictly by their size.

FAN AND FOUNTAIN

Daylily (*Hemerocallis*)
Fountain grass
　　(*Pennisetum alopecuroides*)
Giant feather grass
　　(*Stipa gigantea*)
New Zealand flax
　　(*Phormium tenax*)
Yellow flag
　　(*Iris pseudacorus*)
Yucca
　　(*Yucca filamentosa*)

Front and mid-border plants often display a charming informality. Edge the front of a bed or border using low-growing plants with foliage texture and color that contrast with the lawn or pathway. Lamb's-ear (*Stachys*), with its silver-furred leaves, is a favorite edger. Coral bells (*Heuchera*) is another exquisite choice. First-tier edging plants can form a continuous strip along the garden's front border for a formal effect; however, a combination of various low-growing plants is also pleasing. Alternate clusters of different types of plants to create a subtle edge, but one that clearly states: The garden begins here.

Torch lily makes a striking and unusual mid-border perennial.

HOW TO PLANT BY SHAPE

A potent combination is one that emphasizes contrasts between shape and form. Many designers concentrate on the natural shape of their perennials more than on any other aspect— including color.

You can get the shape you want, of course, by shearing, but that's repetitive work and stresses the plants, too. It's far easier to rely on the innate architecture of the plants, as there is a wide variety of perennial shapes that play especially well against each other. Fans and fountains, mounds and sprawlers, sturdy towers and slim turrets—all can be endlessly recombined into exciting partnerships.

■ Pair a fan-shaped iris with foamy baby's breath. Silky Mexican feather grass (*Stipa tenuissima*) softens look and line, and structural stonecrop (*Sedum spectabile* 'Autumn Joy') adds strength. Striking plants like *Rodgersia pinnata* 'Superba' require equal partners to keep them balanced.
■ Large-scale plants with different textures and colors—for instance, feathery ferns and ligularia—work well. So will large masses of smaller plants, such as hardy geraniums or astilbes (*Astilbe*).
■ Eccentric spires of silvery mullein (*Verbascum chaixii*) become magnificent when placed against large and simple maiden grass (*Miscanthus sinensis*).

SPIKE AND TURRET

Blazing star
　　(*Liatris spicata*)
Bugbane
　　(*Cimicifuga racemosa*)
Delphinium
　　(*Delphinium* × *belladonna*)
Foxglove
　　(*Digitalis purpurea*)
Mullein
　　(*Verbascum chaixii*)
Torch lily
　　(*Kniphophia uvaria*)

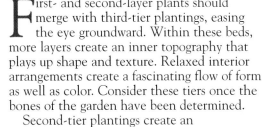

ARCHITECTURAL PLANTS FOR THE PERENNIAL GARDEN

Skyline plantings integrate the garden with surrounding trees or buildings. They enclose the garden and bring it into balance within the scale of its surroundings. Often called "the bones of a garden," well chosen backdrop plantings are not only a supportive framework, they can add floral fireworks all their own.

Big plants create a visual stop, framing bed or border by blocking out distractions such as cars and road signs. Traditional garden design relies on shrubs and trees for the backdrop, but many oversize perennials work well.

In island beds of mixed plantings, the tallest plants need to be toward the center where they don't obscure the shorter plants. In big yards, a hedge of tall ornamental grasses will provide screening, privacy, and a backdrop for flower beds. Pokeweed (*Phytolacca americana*), Joe-Pye weed (*Eupatorium purpureum*), and giant coneflower (*Rudbeckia maxima*), make majestic backdrops, rising tree-like to enclose the yard or garden.

In smaller spaces, a four-foot wall of false indigo (*Baptisia australis*) will provide a natural screen and give you dark blue, pealike flowers in early summer. Airy masses of *Verbena bonariensis* weave into a fine scrim, veiling everything that lies behind it in a shimmering haze of purple-blue clusters.

A shimmering fountain of giant feather grass creates instant architecture.

Add beauty and high drama to the late-summer flower garden with Joe-Pye weed.

THE GARDEN PRIMEVAL

Modern life is full of straight lines and rigid routines, but a garden in which plants dominate and nature rules with its own wild ways is a constant refreshment to the spirit. More and more designers are stressing plant-driven rather than florally-driven gardenscapes. Garden gigantism can give you the opportunity to be utterly embraced by plants. In these new gardens, boldly shaped and oversize plants often play the space-defining role traditionally assigned to hardscaping (walls, trellises, and arbors). But even in the smaller garden, large plants have their place, lending it a surprising sense of the dramatic.

In warm climates where a wide range of true tropical plants flourish, it's easy to give any garden a lush, junglelike appearance. No substitutes are needed; warm climates support the real thing. *Gunnera manicata* and New Zealand flax *(Phormium tenax)* grow to amazing proportions where heat and moisture are in ample supply. Drier hot climates nourish a wide range of astonishing desert plants, including dozens of spurges *(Euphorbia)* as well as broad-bladed grasses and swirling, sword-leaved yuccas.

Mild-winter areas allow hardy tropicals and large-leaved foliage plants to create the impression of jungle abundance yet take moderate frosts in stride. In recent years, plant explorers have increased our palette with dozens of (somewhat) cold-hardy perennial forms of former tropical house plants. Many of these new introductions are finding their way into "Tropicalismo gardens," a school of thought that celebrates joyful gigantism. Characterized by a sense of exuberance, this style features sculptural character with spunky style. Ambitious designers mingle large-scale native plants from their own regions with allies and exotics from all over the world, creating a world-mix of plants that cohabitate with ease.

Plants of prehistoric dimension impose a tropical appearance to the landscape. Some suggestions: ostrich fern (top) thrives in moist shade in a woodland garden, gunnera (center) produces massive leaves, and Chinese rhubarb (bottom) prefers a sheltered border.

BIG, BOLD PLANTS

Cardinal flower *(Lobelia cardinalis)*
Chinese rhubarb *(Rheum palmatum)*
Goatsbeard *(Aruncus dioicus)*
Gunnera *(Gunnera manicata)*
Hosta *(Hosta sieboldiana elegans)*
Joe-Pye weed *(Eupatorium purpureum)*
Ostrich fern *(Matteuccia struthiopteris)*
Pampas grass *(Cortaderia selloana)*
Plume poppy *(Macleaya cordata)*
Pokeweed *(Phytolacca americana)*
Rodgersia *(Rodgersia pinnata)*
Rose mallow *(Hibiscus moscheutos)*
Tatarian aster *(Aster tataricus)*
Zebra grass *(Miscanthus sinensis 'Zebrinus')*

Cold-winter gardeners can create a surprisingly convincing jungle garden by selecting the largest possible members of common perennial families. An enormous clump of zebra grass (top left) boasts splendidly striped foliage. Long-stalked and bronze-tinged rodgersia (top right) is handsome, but one or two plants is all that is required. Hosta sieboldiana elegans (above right) reaches remarkable proportions, with mature plants achieving 5 feet or more in all directions. In the home landscape, big, bold exotic plants in pots and oversized ferns worthy of a prehistoric jungle—combined with cottage garden favorites like delphiniums—create a decidedly tropical feel (right).

PERENNIALS FROM SMALL TO LARGE

Use this chart to help you combine perennials according to size and form. So that you can quickly find a perennial of the correct size you need, at a glance, they are organized in order of their height from short to tall. Each perennial listed is accompanied by a sketch of its typical form, approximately to scale. Remember that this chart is a rough guide; the size given and the form shown can vary according to the cultivar selected, as well as region, weather, and horticultural practice.

Creeping phlox (*Phlox subulata*) 3–6"

Kamtschatka stonecrop (*Sedum kamtschaticum*) 4–9"

Dwarf crested iris (*Iris cristata*) 6"

English primrose (*Primula vulgaris*) 6–9"

Allegheny foam flower (*Tiarella cordifolia*) 6–12"

Sweet violet (*Viola odorata*) 8"

Plumbago (*Ceratostigma plumbaginoides*) 8–12"

Barrenwort (*Epimedium × rubrum*) 8–12"

Fringed bleeding heart (*Dicentra eximia*) 9–18"

Basket-of-gold (*Aurinia saxatilis*) 12"

Yellow corydalis (*Corydalis lutea*) 12"

Japanese painted fern (*Athyrium nipponicum* 'Pictum') 12"

Bergenia (*Bergenia cordifolia*) 12"

Pink (*Dianthus*) 12"

Twinspur (*Diascia*) 12"

Lungwort (*Pulmonaria saccharata*) 12"

'Georgia Blue' speedwell (*Veronica peduncularis* 'Georgia Blue') 12"

Dwarf blue fescue (*Festuca glauca*) 12"

Lamb's-ear (*Stachys byzantina*) 12"

Vial's primrose (*Primula vialii*) 12–15"

Columbine (*Aquilegia*) 1–2'

Marsh marigold (*Caltha palustris*) 12–18"

Fleabane (*Erigeron* hybrids) 1–2'

Lenten rose (*Helleborus orientalis*) 12–18"

Patrinia (*Patrinia scabiosifolia*) 12–18"

Japanese blood grass (*Imperata cylindrica* 'Red Baron') 12–18"

Variegated Japanese sedge (*Carex morrowii* 'Variegata') 12–18"

Hardy geranium (*Geranium*) 1–2'

Maidenhair fern (*Adiantum pedatum*) 12–20"

Golden grass (*Hakonechloa macra* 'Aureola') 1–2'

Creeping verbena (*Verbena* hybrids) 12–18"

Spiked speedwell (*Veronica spicata*) 10–36"

Coral bells (*Heuchera* hybrids) 12-24"

Stoke's aster (*Stokesia laevis*) 12–24"

Lady's mantle (*Alchemilla mollis*) 18"

Threadleaf coreopsis (*Coreopsis verticillata*) 18"

Leopard's bane (*Doronicum orientale*) 18–24"

Geum (*Geum*) 18"

Catmint (*Nepeta × faassenii*) 18–24"

Pincushion flower (*Scabiosa caucasica*) 18–24"

Hardy chrysanthemum (*Chrysanthemum/ Dendranthema* hybrids) 1–3'

Wormwood (*Artemisia ludoviciana*) 2'

Sea holly (*Eryngium amethystinum*) 2'

Crimson pincushion (*Knautia macedonica*) 2'

Shasta daisy (*Leucanthemum × superbum*) 2'

Christmas fern (*Polystichum acrostichoides*) 2'

Japanese primrose (*Primula japonica*) 2'

Stonecrop (*Sedum spectabile*) =(*Hylotelephium spectabile*) 2'

Blanket flower (*Gaillardia × grandiflora*) 2–3'

Beard-tongue (*Penstemon*) 2–3'

Fern-leaf yarrow (*Achillea filipendulina*) 2–3"

Masterwort (*Astrantia major*) 2–3'

Gooseneck lysimachia (*Lysimachia clethroides*) 2–3'

Hybrid sage (*Salvia × sylvestris*) 2–3'

Toad lily (*Tricyrtis hirta*) 2–3'

Peachleaf bellflower (*Campanula persicifolia*) 2–3'

Red valerian (*Centranthus ruber*) 2–3'

Crocosmia (*Crocosmia* hybrids) 2–3'

Hay-scented fern (*Dennstaedtia punctilobula*) 2–3'

Tufted hair grass (*Deschampsia caespitosa*) 2'

Bleeding heart (*Dicentra spectabilis*) 2–3'

Baby's breath (*Gypsophila paniculata*) 2–3'

Daylily (*Hemerocallis*) 1–3'

Bee balm (*Monarda didyma*) 2–3'

Japanese iris (*Iris ensata*) 2–3'

Balloon flower (*Platycodon grandiflorus*) 2–3'

Variegated Solomon's seal (*Polygonatum odoratum* 'Variegatum') 2–3'

Black-eyed Susan (*Rudbeckia fulgida*) 2–3'

Arendsii hybrid astilbe (*Astilbe × arendsii*) 2–4'

Hardy aster (*Aster*) 2–4'

Northern sea oats (*Chasmanthium latifolium*) 30"

Male woodfern (*Dryopteris filix-mas*) 2–4'

Purple coneflower (*Echinacea purpurea*) 2–4'

Bearded iris (*Iris* hybrids) 2–4'

Siberian iris (*Iris siberica*) 2–4'

Purple moor grass (*Molinia caerulea* 'Variegata') 2–4'

Oriental poppy (*Papaver orientale*) 2–4'

Garden phlox (*Phlox paniculata*) 2–4'

Obedient plant (*Physostegia virginiana*) 2–4'

 Japanese anemone (*Anemone × hybrida*) 2–4'

Cushion spurge (*Euphorbia characias*) 3–5'

 **Pokeweed** (*Phytolacca americana*) 4–6'

 Goldenrod (*Solidago* hybrids) 2–4'

 False indigo (*Baptisia australis*) 3–4'

 Monkshood (*Aconitum*) 3–6'

 Joe-Pye weed (*Eupatorium maculatum*) 4–7'

Queen-of-the-prairie (*Filipendula rubra*) 6–8'

 Foxglove (*Digitalis purpurea*) 2–5'

Globe thistle (*Echinops bannaticus*) 3–4'

 Torch lily (*Kniphofia uvaria*) 4'

Hollyhock (*Alcea rosea*) 4–8'

 Meadow rue (*Thalictrum*) 2–6'

 False sunflower (*Heliopsis helianthoides scabra*) 3–4'

 Ostrich fern (*Matteuccia struthiopteris*) 4'

Gunnera (*Gunnera*) 6–10'

Anise hyssop (*Agastache foeniculum*) 3'

 Ligularia (*Ligularia*) 3–4'

 Feather reed grass

Boltonia (*Boltonia asteroides*) 5'

 Blue star (*Amsonia tabernaemontana*) 3'

 Cardinal flower (*Lobelia cardinalis*) 3–4'

(*Calamagrostis × acutiflora* 'Stricta') 4–5'

Ornamental rhubarb (*Rheum palmatum*) 6–10'

 Butterfly weed (*Asclepias tuberosa*) 3'

 Tree mallow (*Lavatera thuringiaca*) 4–5'

 Rose mallow (*Hibiscus moscheutos*) 5'

 **Blue oat grass** (*Helictotrichon sempervirens*) 3'

Hollyhock mallow (*Malva alcea*) 3–4'

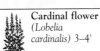 **Frances Williams hosta** (*Hosta sieboldiana* 'Frances Williams') 3'

 Perennial fountain Grass (*Pennisetum alopecuroides*) 3–4'

 Silver spike grass (*Spodiopogon sibiricus*) 4–5'

 **Switch grass** (*Panicum virgatum*) 5'

Plume poppy (*Macleaya cordata*) 8'

 **Blazing star** (*Liatris spicata*) 3'

 Russian sage (*Perovskia atriplicifolia*) 3–4'

 Perennial sunflower (*Helianthus × multiflorus*) 4–6'

 **Giant feather grass** (*Stipa gigantea*) 5'

 Lupine (*Lupinus* 'Russell Hybrid') 3'

 Rogersia (*Rodgersia pinnata*) 3–4'

 Goatsbeard (*Aruncus dioicus*) 4–6'

Maiden grass (*Miscanthus sinensis*) 8'

 Cinnamon fern (*Osmunda cinnamonea*) 3'

 Helen's flower (*Helenium autumnale*) 3–5'

 Bugbane (*Cimicifuga*) 4–6'

 Pampas grass (*Cortaderia selloana*) 5–12'

 Peony (*Paeonia* hybrids) 3'

 Purple loosestrife (*Lythrum salicaria*) 3–5'

 Delphinium (*Delphinium elatum*) 4–6'

 **New Zealand flax** (*Phormium tenax*) 8–10'

 Mullein (*Verbascum chaixii*) 3'

 Yucca (*Yucca filamentosa*) 2–12'

PLAYING WITH COLOR

Purple and yellow repeats in many variations in the garden below, right (and detail right). Textile artists often change primary colors while retaining similar secondary colors in "colorways" (below).

Color brings the garden to life. Flowers and colorful foliage turn the daily greenery of our gardens to a Technicolor harmony. Color stimulates our senses, awakens our emotions, and stirs our sense of beauty. Color work is an art, not a science, and its vocabulary is simple: A *hue* is a pure, saturated color, such as orange or blue. The more saturated it is, the more intense it will appear against a green backdrop. Less saturated colors, such as pastels, recede. A *tone* is either a *shade* (darkened) or a *tint* (lightened) of a pure color. Clean pastel pink, for example, is light and bright; murky red is heavy and dark. Color charts and wheels can help us understand basic color compatibilities, but there are no hard and fast rules because tastes are so personal. After all, some of us

like things subdued; others of us delight in the brazen and enjoy a brilliant clash. The bottom line is that garden color should gladden your spirit and suit your sensibilities.

HOW TO COMBINE COLORS

Use your intuition and fortify it with a few techniques gleaned from artists. Painters and photographers know that light has everything to do with how we perceive color. All day long and into the night, every flower and foliage tint and shade shifts in the slanted light of morning, the floodlight of noon, and the backlight of evening. Position also matters; when light strikes plants set on a bank, it reveals subtones in the foliage—often purple or copper or burgundy—that are masked in massed bed plantings. Indirect or filtered light (what gardeners call high or dappled shade) brings out depths in soft colors that stronger light may bleach.

Companion plants can be partners or competitors, supportive or challenging. Partners chosen for color balance will create harmonies. Competitors will create tension and drama. For example, mix dark orange with spectrum purple and deep, singing red and you'll invoke a western sunset. Sherbet orange blended with chalky yellows and white

looks light and cool, fresh and sparkling. Clean orange and sea blue are midweight colors that balance with each other, while the same orange matched with a red of similar value will edge toward a flamboyant clash (often quite pleasurably). The same clear red looks hotter and brighter against a foliage that is bronze or burgundy, and cooler and darker when set amid pale blue forget-me-nots.

HOW TO CREATE A COLORWAY

Seasonal color alters the garden constantly, from spring's pastels to summer's rainbow, autumn's sunset tints, and winter's green-gray-brown. Develop color themes for each area in the garden or the garden as a whole and repeat those same colors through the seasons. Select compatible colorways (a term borrowed from textile weavers) for the separate areas. When blue is primary, all the other colors are secondary. When yellow replaces blue as primary, blue becomes secondary, and so on. Consult the color chart (pages 32 and 33) to pick your colorways, allowing predominant colors to trade the lead from area to area or season to season, supported by a united family of secondary colors.

A cool palette of violets, pinks, and whites, suggests a colorway with purple as primary while all other colors become secondary (top). A closer look (above) reveals a painterly mixed composition of iris, hardy geranium, delphinium, and beard-tongue.

Variations on a color scheme achieve different effects. The muted pinks and off-whites of a formal setting (above) are tempered with silver artemisia, while bolder pinks and bright white explode from a border (above right).

COLOR AS THEME: WHITE AND COOL

English garden designer Gertrude Jekyll popularized color theme gardens in the early nineteenth century. She was the first to suggest grouping plants that bloom at the same time and insisted that no color can be fully appreciated on its own. Color values are relative, she explained, so any color comes into its own only in relationship to others. A red-theme garden, for instance, would include red's complement, green (its opposite on the color wheel). To make the theme continue through the seasons, flowers with red buds, berries, or red-veined petals and plants that offer new red growth or red fall color would also find a place there. A white garden could contain plants with white or near-white flowers but also contain silvery leaves or white-variegated foliage.

HOW TO WORK WITH WHITE

White can seem difficult to work with but is especially valuable for those who enjoy their gardens in the evenings. It is challenging to match the whites of various flowers, and combinations tend to make off-whites look dingy. Temper the brightness of white flowers with textured foliage plants. Be cautious with pure white; it can be glaring and harsh unless mixed with lustrous greens. Jekyll preferred off-whites—shades she called skim milk, eggshell, or bone, and yellowed tints like butter and cream. Blended with plenty of gray, sage, and olive foliage, these gentle colors weave a sumptuous tapestry. Jekyll thought sticking too closely to a theme was silly. If off-whites look best, or where pale blue, pastel peach, or shell pink will emphasize the cool quality of white, use it! Don't sacrifice effect for strict consistency.

COOLING IT OFF

Colors on the blue side of the spectrum are considered cool, while those on the red side are hot. A palette of soft blues, yellows, and greens yields a cool,

Creamy yellows and saturated purples recede into the landscape, while bursts of frosty peach seem to float (left). Butter yellow lilies support clumps of variegated phlox and dogwood (right).

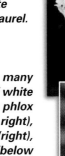

A shimmery blue backyard theme (left) boasts iris, pincushion flower, catmint, lamb's-ears and a pink-white mountain laurel.

The many shades of white include phlox (above right), hellebore (right), foxglove (below right), and goatsbeard (bottom right).

refreshing appearance. Pastel blues and yellows look light and luminous, particularly in the evening. Silvery or blue-gray foliage will emphasize their shimmer, and chartreuse or lime greens will invigorate both blues and purples. Chilly tints of peach with icy apricot, salmon, and chalky yellows with grey and blue foliage make a frosty color scheme.

Matte, muted purple foliage like that of common sage (*Salvia officinalis*), whose fuzzy texture turns it pewtery, is likewise cooling. Almost any pastel tint fits comfortably into cool combinations, whereas pastel shades (grayed or French pastels) work best in warmer schemes.

Be cautious with pure white, it can be harsh unless mixed with textured foliage plants and lustrous greens. White perennials, such as phlox, bugbane (Cimicifuga), wormwood (Artemisia), yarrow (Achillea), and delphinium help illuminate this assemblage of plants.

From dusty pink to bright scarlet, saturated reds demand partners that carry their weight. Rosy sedum anchors a border (left);

vibrant red roses, yarrow, and lupine add depth to a raised bed (center), and masses of red cardinal flower (right) take a stand.

COLOR AS THEME: WARM AND FLAMBOYANT

Cheerful, joyous, ebullient or gaudy, hot colors create instant excitement. Reds, purples, and orange can look brash, brazen or brilliant, depending on how they are assembled. Any combination is bound to be memorable, but unless you want unrestrained riot, it's best to be deliberate. Successful hot combinations will have partners of equal weight and value and significant assistance from surrounding foliage. Screaming orange demands a dazzling red. Soft pink will look insignificant. When the main colors—perhaps plum purple and apple red—are both saturated, dark green foliage will anchor them firmly. Rich, deep reds and purples can disappear into the background. Lighter reds mixed with shocking pinks and purples will make those murky colors sing, especially with a lift of chartreuse

Heat up the garden with yellow torch lily (above left), orange butterfly weed (left), and red chrysanthemum (below left).

A flamboyant display (right) includes a bold combination of orange torch lily, scarlet dahlia, red bee balm, and both yellow yarrow and black-eyed Susan.

Repeated vignettes carry a color theme throughout the perennial border. Ornamental grasses (left) and clumps of yellow bloomers (right) extend as far as the eye can see.

foliage. Silver, gray, and blue-green foliage make darker oranges and smudgy reds volcanic. Purple and blue leaves lend weight and depth to bright oranges and fresh greens, high colors that seem to float on their own.

HOW TO DEVELOP A THEME

In choosing the palette for your garden, consider the overall effect you want to achieve; solid sheets of unbroken color work well in larger landscapes but seem relentless in smaller gardens, especially when many of your plants are long bloomers. It's most effective to repeat colorful vignettes—small groups of related color plants—throughout the entire garden. For multiseason color, give each vignette some spring, summer, autumn, and even winter performers. In formal settings, space these repetitions precisely. Remember, cottage or naturalistic gardens call for informality. And avoid a boring sameness; vary form and height and mass and texture within your color groupings themselves.

Foliage contrasts in chartreuse and burgundy maintain visual interest with loads of texture and little emphasis on blossom (left). Deep purples seem to recede in the border, allowing texture and structure to dominate (right).

Golden creeping Jenny provides an electrifying foil for clumps of burgundy-leaved coral bells, spikes of lily foliage, and a host of textures (above), including bugleweed, hardy geranium, and beard-tongue.

PAINTING WITH FOLIAGE

We generally begin our gardening because we fall for flowers, but as we continue gardening our appreciation for foliage increases as well. It's obvious that nature loves green. It is the most common color in the plant world—the basic black of gardening—and it's not often thought of when we choose our plants. There are a thousand shades of green. They can give the garden body and depth and can be used in the palette just like any other colors.

What's more, foliage presents us with hundreds of alternatives to basic green. Strikingly beautiful gardens can be made simply by combining green foliage with blue- and gold-, silver- and bronze-, or red- and purple-leaved plants. Harmonious or contrasting foliage can be combined even more readily than flowers, and it persists far longer. Luminous or softly gilded foliage will brighten a shady corner. Stronger sun brings out hidden undertones in deep colored foliage and strengthens the flush of fall. Leaves present us with a remarkable range of shape and size as well as texture and finish.

Perennial foliage offers us the opportunity to develop stunning seasonal effects, starting with earliest spring. Peonies (*Paeonia*) produce copper red new leaves atop black or

A variety of colors and textures are combined in a mixed border (above) both for depth and added visual interest. Note how the darker shades set off and strengthen the lighter foliage plantings as well as the blossoms of the yellow tickseed, the purple hardy geraniums, and spikes of yellow torch lily.

burgundy stems. Certain hardy geraniums have hot red new leaves, while many spurges (*Euphorbia*) emerge sizzling chartreuse, glowing orange, or frosty purple. In fall, the clear gold of balloon flower (*Platycodon grandiflorus*) foliage, the shocking pink of beard-tongue (*Penstemon*), the ember red of plumbago (*Ceratostigma plumbaginoides*) all contribute to the garden's gaiety.

HOW TO USE VARIEGATION

Variegated foliage lightens and brightens the garden tapestry, and strikingly variegated shade plants can illuminate dark spaces.

■ Choose somewhat simple patterns—perhaps an edging of cream or pink or yellow—and large, restful leaves.

■ Powerfully patterned plants can lend focus to a jumble and can elevate a dull planting to high art. (They may create visual chaos if mixed with more enthusiasm than care. If your vignettes have become overly variegated, add plain plants with large, simple leaves.)

■ Many variegated leaves scorch in full sun, yet most need adequate light to develop their best coloration. The answer is to place them where they receive plenty of indirect, filtered or diffused light. Morning sun rarely burns foliage, and where high shade is scarce, planting on the north side of tall companions will create pockets of afternoon shade.

Plants with variegated foliage enliven shady woodland settings (left). Repeated clumps of striped golden grass (Hakonechloa) reflect light into the garden and soften the stone risers that lead to an inviting seat.

Finely textured ferns, bold-leaved hostas, and a variety of mixed plants combine to create a visual potpourri in a remarkably layered shade garden (below).

TOP 10 VARIEGATED PERENNIALS

Coral bells (*Heuchera* 'Ruby Veil')

Japanese painted fern (*Athyrium nipponicum* 'Pictum')

Bethlehem sage (*Pulmonaria saccharata* 'Benediction')

Maiden grass (*Miscanthus sinensis* 'Morning Light')

Hosta (*Hosta* 'Great Expectations')

Solomon seal (*Polygonatum odoratum* 'Variegatum')

Yellow flag iris (*Iris pseudacorus* 'Variegata')

Yucca (*Yucca filamentosa* 'Golden Sword')

Look up close at any old master portrait, like The Clown with the Lute *by Frans Hals (above), and you'll see many surprising tints. Use this idea to create transitions in the garden.*

Ornamental grasses come in an array of sizes, shapes, and colors, making them marvelous mixers (below left), backdrops (below center), and accents (below right).

BLEND COLORS LIKE A MASTER PAINTER

When we shop for plants, those with clear, bright coloration are the first to catch our eye. If we are shopping with a color theme in mind, we will naturally tend to select plants that fit within its parameters. However, there are myriad subtle, in-between tones that—though they are less likely to catch our eye—will lend a painterly quality to our color work. Close inspection of

any old master portrait will reveal a dozen such tints in any inch of canvas. Under the subject's eyes, around the mouth, there are smeary greens and pallid grays that mingle with orange or yellow. Up close, they look ugly, but seen as a whole, the composition resolves these smears and bits and globs into an image of potent beauty. The lesson here is that there are no bad colors, and we can place the blending colors and achieve results similar to that of the master painters.

HOW TO WORK WITH STRONG COLORS

Blending colors come in two large groups, which can be loosely described as pale or deep. Use them to merge stronger colors; their blending tones make gentle transitions from one to the next. Pale tints lend brilliance and sparkle to deep-toned compositions. Tints of milk and cream, butter and bone will brighten anything from midnight blue and purple to searing reds and oranges, as well as dainty pastel combinations.

In stronger colored compositions, bright pastels, such as peach and salmon, canary and chalk yellow, sand and chamois, buff and biscuit will lighten the heaviness of hot or sullen colors. Deep shades add depth to colorful but unsaturated combinations that "float" or seem unpleasantly brash. Murky mixers such as mahogany and port, tobacco and cordovan are retreating colors, yet these shades add weight to bright combinations. Smudgy shades can intensify contrast, making vivid colors more brilliant and lifting soft

ones from obscurity into prominence.

Just as in an old master portrait, well-chosen intermediate shades mellow the harsh, meld the otherwise incompatible, and create transitions between areas with different color themes. Foliage plants are excellent. Each has its own texture, gloss or matte, which dresses up not only its own appearance but that of its neighbors. Use foliage plants as mixer plants in small amounts, as accents and as echoes. Unlike plants used to state the gardener's theme, use mixers sparingly and with an eye to the overall effect of the composition.

HOW TO FIND THE RIGHT BLENDERS

Many a brash garden scheme simply needs toning down with blenders so it scintillates rather than shocks. To find effective blenders, take flower and foliage samples from each main player in an unsatisfying composition to a good nursery. Use them to find plants that create links between seemingly incompatible colors. Color changers, plants whose foliage alters in different lights, help relate the warriors. For example, blue-green spurges (*Euphorbia*) may offer tints of copper or mahogany that will awaken color echoes between hot and cool tones. Purple-leaved perennials such as loosestrife (*Lysimachia punctata*) appear bronze and almost orange in some lights and smoky purple in others.

To illustrate the concept of proper color blending with flower and foliage, the receding shadows and forward-seeming highlights have been removed from this garden image (top). The shadows represent the retreating colors; the highlights represent the bolder ones. Note how flat and unsatisfying the border now appears. With the highlights restored (center), their role in building relief with darker plants becomes more obvious. And finally, with both shadows and highlights restored (bottom), the setting has mellowed into a satisfying composition; the shadows and highlights bridge easy transitions between seemingly incompatible color areas.

ORGANIZING COLOR: THE WARM RANGE

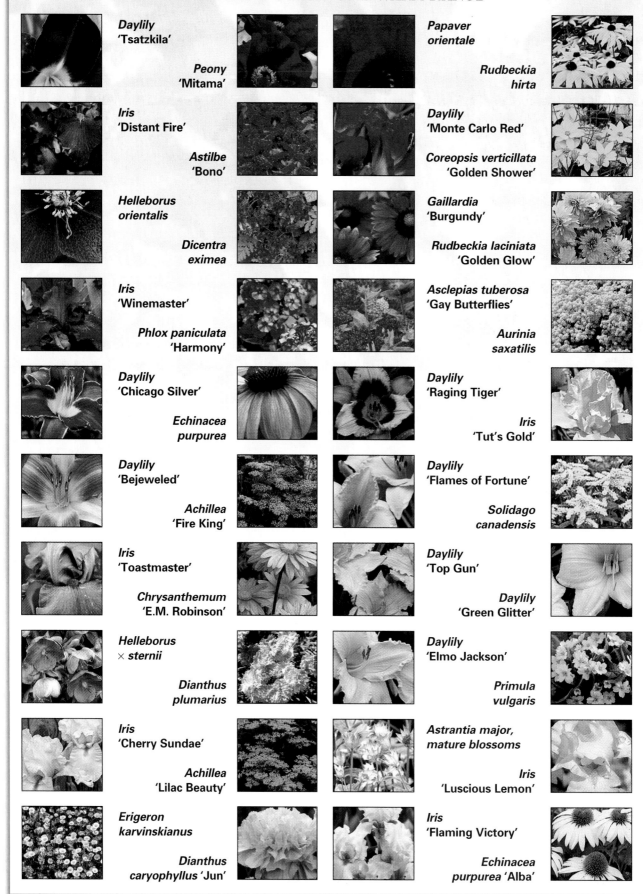

Daylily 'Tsatzkila'

Peony 'Mitama'

Papaver orientale

Rudbeckia hirta

Iris 'Distant Fire'

Astilbe 'Bono'

Daylily 'Monte Carlo Red'

Coreopsis verticillata 'Golden Shower'

Helleborus orientalis

Dicentra eximea

Gaillardia 'Burgundy'

Rudbeckia laciniata 'Golden Glow'

Iris 'Winemaster'

Phlox paniculata 'Harmony'

Asclepias tuberosa 'Gay Butterflies'

Aurinia saxatilis

Daylily 'Chicago Silver'

Echinacea purpurea

Daylily 'Raging Tiger'

Iris 'Tut's Gold'

Daylily 'Bejeweled'

Achillea 'Fire King'

Daylily 'Flames of Fortune'

Solidago canadensis

Iris 'Toastmaster'

Chrysanthemum 'E.M. Robinson'

Daylily 'Top Gun'

Daylily 'Green Glitter'

Helleborus × sternii

Dianthus plumarius

Daylily 'Elmo Jackson'

Primula vulgaris

Iris 'Cherry Sundae'

Achillea 'Lilac Beauty'

Astrantia major, mature blossoms

Iris 'Luscious Lemon'

Erigeron karvinskianus

Dianthus caryophyllus 'Jun'

Iris 'Flaming Victory'

Echinacea purpurea 'Alba'

ORGANIZING COLOR: THE COOL RANGE

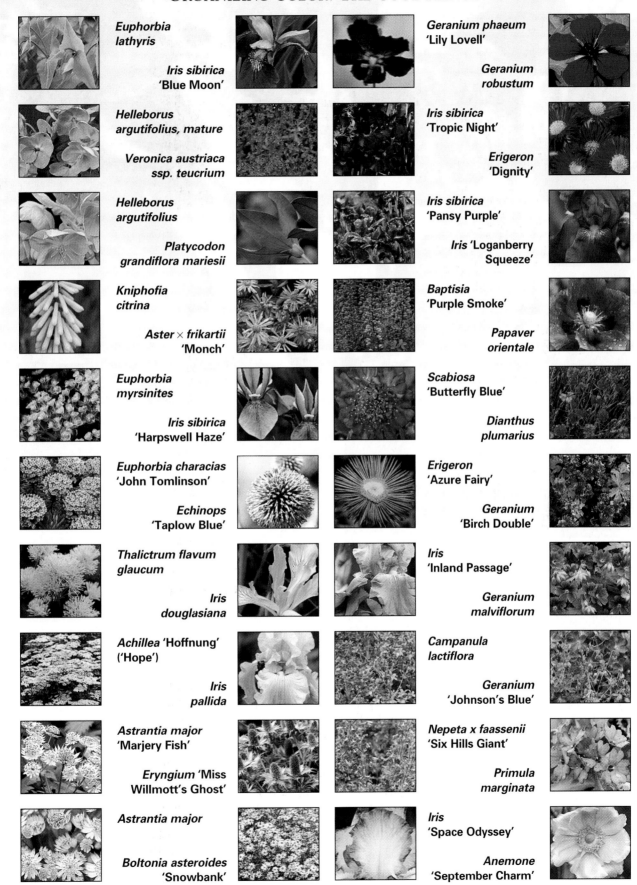

Euphorbia lathyris

Iris sibirica 'Blue Moon'

Helleborus argutifolius, mature

Veronica austriaca ssp. teucrium

Helleborus argutifolius

Platycodon grandiflora mariesii

Kniphofia citrina

Aster × *frikartii* 'Monch'

Euphorbia myrsinites

Iris sibirica 'Harpswell Haze'

Euphorbia characias 'John Tomlinson'

Echinops 'Taplow Blue'

Thalictrum flavum glaucum

Iris douglasiana

Achillea 'Hoffnung' ('Hope')

Iris pallida

Astrantia major 'Marjery Fish'

Eryngium 'Miss Willmott's Ghost'

Astrantia major

Boltonia asteroides 'Snowbank'

Geranium phaeum 'Lily Lovell'

Geranium robustum

Iris sibirica 'Tropic Night'

Erigeron 'Dignity'

Iris sibirica 'Pansy Purple'

Iris 'Loganberry Squeeze'

Baptisia 'Purple Smoke'

Papaver orientale

Scabiosa 'Butterfly Blue'

Dianthus plumarius

Erigeron 'Azure Fairy'

Geranium 'Birch Double'

Iris 'Inland Passage'

Geranium malviflorum

Campanula lactiflora

Geranium 'Johnson's Blue'

Nepeta x faassenii 'Six Hills Giant'

Primula marginata

Iris 'Space Odyssey'

Anemone 'September Charm'

GROWING
PERENNIALS

Discover new and unusual regional plants for the garden at local plant sales or a swap sponsored by an arboretum or plant society.

FINDING THE RIGHT PLANT FOR THE RIGHT PLACE

Which perennials will grow best for you depends in good part upon the climate of the region in which you live. Climate, in fact, may be the single most critical factor in your gardening success.

Before you purchase your perennials, do a little research. You need to know the cold hardiness zone for your region (see the USDA map on page 96). If a plant is listed in a catalog or in the Selection Guide (pages 46 to 91) as hardy to your area—it means it will likely survive winters where you live.

Cold hardiness, however, is only one aspect of climate. A plant listed as hardy to zone 8, for example, will survive winters in both Atlanta and Portland. However, it may thrive in a Portland summer but may not do well at all in southern heat. Some sources, including the Selection Guide, will list hardiness zones in a range. If your favorite perennial choices are designated as hardy in zones 4 to 7, for example, they will survive winters in zone 4 (and regions that are warmer) and generally do well in summers in zone 7 (and cooler).

Within zones, there are conditions other than temperature to consider. The high humidity of the South, for example, can be as challenging to perennials as the heat. So can clay or sandy soils. Humidity invites insects and diseases, and extreme soil conditions can cause plants to get too much or too little water. You can, however, choose perennials that adapt to these conditions.

In the Southwest, the dry air may be the challenge. Rainfall can be sparse, and water may be restricted. Heat-, drought-, and cold-resistant plants (to cope with plummeting nightfall temperatures) will improve your gardening success. Alkaline desert soils may need amendments to make them more acid.

Far northern gardeners (and their perennials) face bone-chilling winter cold, and frost as late as June and as early as August. Many perennials will survive these winters, and there are ways to get around the realities of the cold. Choose perennials that bloom when frost is not likely. Keep this information in hand before purchasing plants and be sure to jot it down in your journal.

Next, inventory your garden for its microclimates. These are small pockets where temperatures, soil conditions, drainage, and light vary not only from the average in your landscape but from each other as well.

An open area, for example, might be windier than others; low spots can keep the frost and won't drain after rain or watering. Areas shaded by trees or shrubs or that lie in the shadow of the house may stay cooler.

WHERE TO BUY PERENNIALS

Finding perennials can be as simple as taking a trip to the nearest garden center. Plants will generally be available in 4-inch pots or gallon containers. With a good selection of attractive, well-rooted plants, you're in luck. Choose vigorous plants with plenty of lush new growth. Avoid limp, brittle, puckered, or discolored foliage, which may be symptoms of stress or disease.

Happy, well-grown plants have sturdy stems and sit firmly in their pots. Poorly rooted ones may teeter, and their anchor roots may be partially exposed above the soil level. A small but sturdy plant is preferable to a larger one that's lank and flopping. A few roots poking from the bottom of a plant can mean the plant is raring to go, but if you suspect a plant is root bound, turn it carefully out of its pot (or ask the nursery staff to do it for you) and take a look. Healthy roots make a solid web through which you can still detect some soil. A solid mass of tightly wound roots means the plant has been waiting too long.

You may also find perennials as first-year seedlings planted in plastic cells (usually six to a pack). Six-pack perennials are much less expensive than their container-grown counterparts, but remember you may have to wait an additional year for a good display.

HOW TO GARDEN BY MAIL

Plants raised in your region will adapt better to your garden than those grown elsewhere, but local-nursery selections may be limited. For that specialty plant you simply can't do without, you can turn to garden clubs, plant societies, or mail-order sources. Mail-order houses will mail both their catalogs and your selections early enough to make your choices and get them planted. You can use the Source List on page 93 to find reliable mail-order sources.

A catalog order will arrive as either a dormant bare root plant (with roots protected in a moist medium) or as a potted plant. It's best to plant bare-root perennials (or any purchase for that matter) as soon as possible, but you can store them for a week before planting if you keep them moist and cool.

How many plants to buy? If you aren't in a hurry, buy single plants of each of your favorites and divide them often. Given good conditions, small plants fatten up fast, providing plenty of divisions each season. If you need a lot of plants, growing from seed offers an attractive alternative to blowing the budget. Many perennials are easy to grow from seed, which offers you an opportunity to grow varieties not otherwise available.

Mail-order plants usually arrive as dormant plants with bare roots enclosed in sphagnum moss and wrapped in plastic (above left), or as potted plants with the top growth visible (above right). Find a nursery that carries a wide selection of plants (below). Container-grown plants (inset) have adapted to confined quarters, and their roots may be growing in circles.

SOIL BUILDING

Perennials can provide outstanding effect in short order. Shown above in only its second season, this new border was developed using the easy technique described on page 37.

Whether your perennials survive depends on climate. Whether they thrive depends on soil conditions, nutrient levels, soil pH (a measure of its acidity or alkalinity), and, of course, water.

An ideal soil will have a mix of its major ingredients—sand, silt, and clay—in proportions (of roughly a third each) that will let air and water pass through but will retain enough nutrients to support active plant growth. Balanced plant growth and strong roots, in turn, require balanced feeding.

HOW TO MAKE SOIL FOR CONTAINERS

Plants in pots need especially good soil because they are subject to drying, heating, cooling, and leaching of nutrients. You can mix your own potting soil or buy it. The goal is a medium that holds water well so you don't have to water constantly, drains well so roots get enough oxygen, supports plants so they don't flop over, and provides a slow-release source of phosphorus and potassium. Potting mixes usually contain some of the following ingredients: compost or leaf mold, peat moss, sand, soil (loam or commercial potting soil), perlite, vermiculite, bonemeal, granite dust, greensand, langbeinite, sulfur, or limestone. If you buy a soilless mix— one that contains perlite, vermiculite, and peat, but no actual soil or sand—add 1 part good, loamy, crumbly garden soil or commercial potting soil for every 5 parts soilless mix. The soil is a buffer against changes in nutrient levels and pH.

Wise gardeners say, "Grow flowers hard and vegetables soft." They treat vegetables to every nutritional luxury, since any shortage may reduce the harvest. In contrast, they put perennials on a leaner diet to produce the best flowers. Optimal perennial growth depends on strong root systems. Well-fed plants are well-rooted; they withstand drought, wild weather, pests, and disease better than those with shallow roots.

HOW TO FERTILIZE PLANTS

The building blocks of plant nutrition are nitrogen, phosphorus, and potassium. These essential soil elements (represented by the letters N, P, K on fertilizer labels) are the plant-world equivalent of proteins, fats, and carbohydrates. Secondary and trace elements (like calcium, manganese, chlorine, and iron) act like vitamin and mineral supplements. Nitrogen is the leaf builder; with trace elements it creates the proteins of green tissue. Phosphorus promotes flowering, and potassium strengthens roots. Even if ample nutrients are present, plants won't be able to absorb them unless the soil pH is neutral (6.5 to 7.5 on a 14-point scale) or slightly acid (5.5 to 6.5).

Most perennials will tolerate and adapt to a range of soil conditions, nutrients, and pH levels that are less than ideal, but you may want to enlist the aid of your cooperative extension agent or a private laboratory for a soil test. Test results will tell you about your soil and recommend amendments if needed.

There are a number of materials you can use to amend the texture of your soil, but perhaps the most valuable is organic matter. Organic amendments, such as compost, aged manure, and other natural materials, break down into humus, which opens tight soils and makes sandy soils more water and nutrient retentive. (In heavy clay soils, add builder's sand or gypsum to improve drainage.)

Soils that are nutritionally lean, especially those deficient in nitrogen, can be enriched with soy- and cottonseed meals or other organic fertilizers, but give organic fertilizers adequate time and temperature (four weeks at 50° to 60° F) to work before planting. Aged manure and alfalfa pellets, which work together to release extra nitrogen, don't take as much time. Synthetic fertilizers are the fastest (but require more frequent applications) than organic nutrients.

If your soil pH needs balancing more than is possible with organic matter (which is generally pH neutral), use agricultural lime to sweeten it (make it less acid) and sulphur or ferrous sulphate to make it less alkaline. A pine-needle mulch acidifies well, also.

HOW TO BUILD AN EASY BED

Once you've established your soil conditions and determined which amendments it needs, the next step is to decide what kind of bed to make for your perennials. Ground-level or raised beds are your options. (In either case, you can prepare the bed in the spring, but it's better done in the fall).

To make a ground-level bed, you'll have to first remove the sod with a sod cutter (which you can rent) or by sliding a spade under the roots. Spread organic matter (2 to 6 inches deep), fertilizer (with a 5-10-5 analysis, 3 to 5 pounds per 100 square feet) and pH amendments and till them into the soil to a depth of 6 to 12 inches.

You may find making a raised bed easier. It accomplishes all requirements of soil texture, fertility, and pH, and requires no tilling. In effect, you're making your own soil; you can skip the soil-testing step, and you don't have to consider amendments. Here's how to build an easy bed right on top of your lawn:

■ Start with a base of sandy loam, 8 to 12 inches deep (you can purchase sandy loam at builders' supply stores). Unless the garden site is extremely weedy, underlying grass need not be removed.

■ Add a thick (6- to 8-inch) layer of compost or aged manure, mounding it smoothly. There is no need to till the beds.

■ Simply prepare each planting hole individually, mixing the loam and compost or manure before placing the new plant. Dairy manure or compost is a better top dressing and mulch choice than peat, which is extremely difficult to rewet when dry.

A thick blanket of manure conserves moisture, helps keep beds weed free, and looks tidy. Over time, earthworms will incorporate the loam and manure, so add an annual 2- to 3-inch top dressing of manure or compost mulch.

No More Double-Digging!

Build a perennial bed in three easy steps. There's no need to mix the beds since earthworms will incorporate the loam and manure over time. Landscape fabric, (sometimes called weed-barrier cloth) keeps paths weed free.

Step 1: Start by laying weed-barrier cloth along the paths. Spread sandy loam 8 to 12 inches deep on top of bed area.

Step 2: Add a 6- to 8-inch layer of compost or aged manure, mounding it smoothly. No need to till.

Step 3: Cover the edges of the weed-barrier cloth with soil, then cover the path with gravel to hold cloth in place.

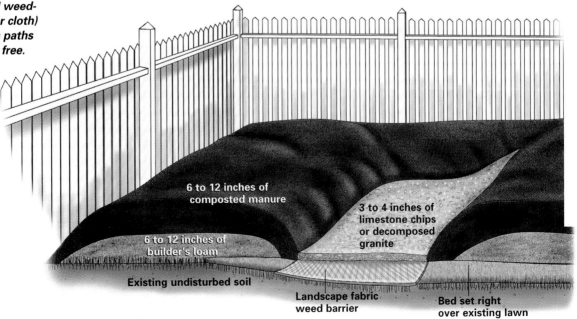

6 to 12 inches of composted manure

6 to 12 inches of builder's loam

3 to 4 inches of limestone chips or decomposed granite

Existing undisturbed soil

Landscape fabric weed barrier

Bed set right over existing lawn

PLANTING PERENNIALS

Placement and planting go hand in hand—they are the keys to a healthy and handsome garden. Before you plant, consider the relative vigor and ultimate size of each perennial. In a well-filled border, neighboring plants barely touch; they weave a tapestry that looks unbroken but allows air to freely circulate. To create a more generous look, start young plants close and move them as they mature. You may find it useful to stake the location of your plants before setting them in. Wait for a cloudy day, especially if your plants are bare-root plants. New roots dry out quickly in the sun, so water well.

In the North, it's best to plant bare-root perennials in the spring. In zones 5 and warmer, spring or fall planting is equally good. With few exceptions, container-grown plants can be planted anytime during the season when the ground can be worked—early enough in autumn to become established before the first frost.

There are slight differences in planting methods for bare-root and container-grown perennials, but in each case, dig the hole as deep as the root lengths and about a third wider than the root spread. In an established bed, blend the removed soil with an equal amount of compost or aged manure.

For bare-root plants, fill the hole halfway, making a conical mound in the center. Loosen the roots with your fingers, cut off any dead, damaged, or diseased roots, and fan them out over the mound. Sprinkle soil over them and firm it with your hands, making sure the crown stays at the soil level. If your plant is taprooted (one with a single long root), you won't need as big a hole or mound. Use a trowel to make a narrow hole as deep as the root, plant it with its crown at soil level, and tamp the soil firmly.

CONTAINER-GROWN PLANTS

Container-grown plants are easier. Follow the old adage that says dig a gallon hole for a 4-inch pot. Mix the soil as you would for a bare-root plant, and remove the pot. Turn it upside down with one hand spread over the soil. Tap or squeeze the pot gently until the plant comes loose from the container.

Dig holes large enough so that roots won't be cramped when they are spread out (below). The depth of the hole is determined by the roots of the plant. The point where the roots meet the stem (the crown) should be placed right at ground level.

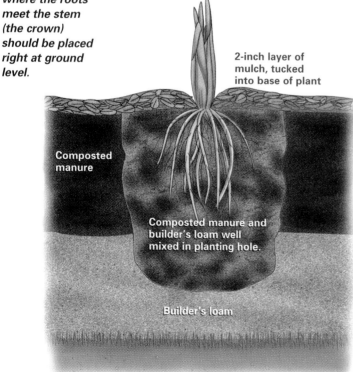

2-inch layer of mulch, tucked into base of plant

Composted manure

Composted manure and builder's loam well mixed in planting hole.

Builder's loam

Clip off any roots that are broken, dry, brittle, or rotted (top), then get the plant into the ground as quickly as possible (bottom).

Container-grown plants may have roots growing in circles. To help, tease any bound roots or quarter the root ball (cut it in fourths from the bottom with a sharp knife to about half its depth). A few perennials, such as bleeding heart (*Dicentra*), have brittle roots, but most are very sturdy, so don't worry about hurting them. Spread the quarters and plant with the crown at soil level.

If you're working with plants in six-packs, dig holes about the same depth as the root ball and plant them at the same depth as in the container. Don't pull them out of the pack by their stems—push them out from the bottom. Finish your planting by watering thoroughly and renewing the mulch or top dressing. Water every day for the first week or two until the plants become established.

How to Stake Perennials

Even if you've selected sturdy, self-supporting plants, some of them will need unobtrusive staking to stand tall. Where heavy summer rains are common, staking will prevent or minimize the collapse of your prized delphiniums. In exposed, windy gardens, many others will be better off with staking. There are dozens of ways to keep plants upright, from simple webs of sticks and string to expensive hoops and linking systems. The goal is always the same: to design effective but nearly invisible supports. Install them in early spring, long before the need is obvious.

TRADITIONAL STAKING

For long-stemmed plants like delphinium, give each blooming stem its own stake. Use a stake that is a foot longer than the expected stem

height. Place it 5 to 6 inches out from the plant crown to avoid damaging the roots. Sink it at least a foot into the ground (use a rubber mallet) so the portion above ground is almost as tall as the stem will be. Secure the stem to the stake as it grows, tying it every 12 to 18 inches of new growth. Thick, green, or black bamboo wands are sturdy and inconspicuous but short-lived. Slim steel rebar is even stronger, lasts forever, and its dull silver soon turns rusty brown that disappears like camouflage into the background.

OTHER SUPPORTS

Mounding plants such as peony (*Paeonia*) and aster splay open when wet, but short-legged border hoops placed around the base of the plants will help keep them upright and

properly in place. Tall monkshood (*Aconitum*) and mullein (*Verbascum*) look unnaturally stiff if tied to stakes, so use tomato cages woven with twiggy willow strands to disguise the shiny metal. A short row of linked stakes will keep tall, arching crocosmias in line. Give shorter, floppy plants a supportive hoop skirt of pea sticks (stout, twiggy branches cut from fruit trees, hazel, or alder) set firmly into the ground near their crowns. When unstaked plants start to tumble, prevent disaster by weaving cats cradles of dark-colored string between the stems, anchoring the makeshift web to several short but stout stakes. Remember to make a note in your garden journal to remind yourself to stake that tumbling plant next spring.

One simple method is to use a bamboo pole or rebar driven into the ground. Tie a single-stem plant to the stake with string, fabric, or a plant tie.

Grow-through supports or hoops are positioned over a plant while it is young. Stems and leaves grow through it, hiding the support.

A series of metal plant stakes coated with green plastic can be used to prop up flopping blossoms, keeping garden pathways tidy.

Plants with numerous stems can be supported by driving several stakes into the ground and connecting them with natural-color twine.

Organic fertilizers, such as alfalfa pellets (above), are derived from minerals, animals, and plants. They release nutrients slowly, through the action of soil organisms. Chemical fertilizers are more concentrated.

CARING FOR PERENNIALS

Keeping well-chosen and properly placed and planted perennials happy is not difficult. Plants whose essential needs are met remain content with only moderate care. Newly planted perennials must be kept adequately moist for their entire first season, but once established, many are relatively drought tolerant.

How do you tell if the plants need water? Dig down 3 to 4 inches. If the soil is dry at this depth, water thoroughly, then let the soil dry before watering again. It's best to do your watering in the morning to give the foliage time to dry (foliage that remains damp in the evening invites disease). Consider using a soaker hose or drip irrigation; either will deliver water directly to the roots and saturate the soil directly instead of running off.

You can reduce your watering needs with a deep (2- to 4-inch) layer of aged manure or compost mulch, renewed each spring and fall. Mulches conserve moisture, suppress weeds, and supply a measure of protection from frost and heaving. Plastic mulches (or even newspaper) will work, but organic mulches break down and add valuable humus to the soil. Supplement the organic blend with alfalfa pellets in the spring and soy or cottonseed meal in fall; this feeding mulch will supply your perennials with all the nutrients they need—in a slow, steady diet.

Plants nursery raised with a liquid fertilizer may need spot feeding during their first season. If they dwindle after planting, give them a half-strength dose of 5-10-5 liquid fertilizer. (Use a watering can for spot feeding in small gardens and an in-hose sprayer for larger beds.) Most will gain back their lost looks in a few days. Once established, nearly all perennials will be satisfied with a twice yearly feeding mulch.

To promote extra bloom, however, begin weekly liquid feedings of a balanced 20-20-20 fertilizer in late spring. And remember when using this or any fertilizer to make sure the soil is moist—even half-strength fertilizers can burn dry roots.

HOW TO GROOM PROPERLY

Grooming is a constant chore, but the more often performed, the lighter the task. Make tidiness your goal, not prissy perfection. Daily or weekly, removing spent flowers and damaged or browning foliage keeps the garden pleasantly tidy and the gardener aware of its state and subtle changes.

There are four grooming practices—in addition to generally picking up—and each has its own purposes.

■ **THINNING**—involves spring removal at ground level of some of the stems of bushy plants. Thinning lets the light in and the air circulate and helps prevent mildew.

■ **PINCHING**—at the tips of stems—makes leggy plants more compact, because side branches with new blooms will grow where you've pinched it back. Begin in late spring or early summer, pinching every week or so.

■ **DISBUDDING**—pinching out smaller buds—will give you larger blooms on plants such as peonies (*Paeonia*) and roses.

■ **DEADHEADING**—removing faded flowers—will stimulate long and repeated bloom in many perennials. In general, cut the flower stems back to the next set of leaves; that's where side shoots and buds are waiting to make new bloom.

As autumn draws near, increase your grooming. If you have messy floppers, trim them back. But allow the upright grasses and statuesque perennials to remain in place so you can see which ones hold their dramatic effect into the winter season.

Be vigilant; problems solved quickly remain minor. Look for yellowing or puckered foliage, stunted growth, and buds that rot before they open. These are common symptoms of health problems and may be caused by crowding, compacted soil, or poor planting. Alter the condition to correct the problem. Discard or burn seriously diseased plants (never put them on the compost heap, where they may spread trouble). You can control most insect damage with a quick blast from the hose or a dose of insecticidal soap, but if intractable problems develop, dig up the suffering plant and check the roots. When one plant suffers while others thrive, the culprit is often root damage.

Edit your selections as well and be ready for some surprises. No matter how thoroughly your research has been or careful your selection, your perennials may behave differently than you thought they would.

After perennials bloom, cut off faded flowers (left) unless they will produce decorative seed heads. Deadheading keeps the garden neat and encourages reblooming.

If certain plants outgrow their allotted space before their companions can catch up, remove them to restore the relationship you had in mind. Get rid of slackers, too—those that fail to perform and don't respond to feeding or extra care. Be judicious when planting their replacements (there's no point in replanting one problem with another) but never hesitate to take a few risks. Gardening is an art rather than a science, and gardeners learn best through trial and error.

Allow seed heads to form on perennials such as stonecrop and black-eyed Susan (below) for winter interest and as a source of food for the birds.

MAKING MORE

Most perennials are easy to propagate by a process called division—splitting a large plant into smaller ones. A single mature plant can provide plenty of offspring to fill new beds or trade with friends. Indeed, perennials that are strong growers require periodic division to stay healthy. Daylily (*Hemerocallis*), hosta, and Siberian iris (*Iris sibirica*), for example, become congested and bloom poorly unless divided regularly, generally every third year. Baby's breath (*Gypsophila paniculata*), and red valerian (*Centranthus ruber*) can be left alone for many years until scanty blooms or scrawny stems signal the need for division. A few perennials, such as the popular tickseed (*Coreopsis*), must be divided each season for best performance.

As a general rule, divide fast growers every two or three years, before they become too bulky to handle easily. Slower growers need only be divided when they outgrow their position. But exercise caution: If a mature perennial starts to bloom sparsely or has small foliage, it may be ready to divide. But it may only need feeding (with a half-strength fertilizer) or treatment for disease. If the condition persists, it's time for surgery.

HOW TO DIVIDE PERENNIALS

Division is most commonly performed in spring or fall, depending on your region. In cold climates, divide and replant in early fall or spring. Elsewhere, fall division is best. As a rule of thumb, divide early bloomers late and late bloomers early. There are a few basic techniques for division, depending on root type. All begin by digging up the mother plant and shaking off excess soil. Clumping plants with multiple crowns, such as daylily and hosta, can be teased apart when young. But older plants must be sliced apart and smaller pieces shaken loose. Border and Siberian iris have plump storage roots called rhizomes, which snap into pieces. In order to grow on, each bit of root must have an "eye" (growth point) or an intact tuft of foliage.

HOW TO GROW PERENNIALS FROM SEED

Anybody who has successfully grown vegetables, herbs, or annual flowers from seed will have no trouble growing popular perennials this way. A few perennials have specific requirements (perhaps needing light or a period of chilling to germinate), which will nearly always be noted on the seed packets. In general, it's wise to sow fresh seed as promptly as possible. Most perennials germinate best when overwintered outdoors, though placement in a cold frame is a good idea where winters are very cold. In spring, the emerging plants can be potted up into 4-inch containers. Many perennials prefer to move into larger-size containers more slowly and may even die off if over-potted. Let the roots be your guide: Some plants may need two full years before they are ready to be potted into gallons or the open garden. Others will produce huge root systems right away, signaling their immediate need for roomier quarters.

Divide Perennials in Three Easy Steps

Step 1: *A practiced foot is often your best division tool. Step down firmly on a sharp spade to split an older root system into two halves.*

Step 2: *Two spading forks work best to divide perennials with a massive root system, such as this hosta. Remove old and tough roots.*

Step 3: *Depending on the size of the plant, use an edger to cut three or more divisions. Replant each clump immediately in a fresh hole.*

HOW TO MAKE WILLOW WATER

To encourage the rooting of stem cuttings, just after making a cutting, dip it in willow water, a homemade substance that contains natural rooting hormones. To make willow water, cut short sticks (a foot or two long) from any kind of willow and place them, cut side down, in a bucket of water. After a week or so, you can use the water (now faintly tea-colored) as a dip for your cuttings. Keep it fresh by recutting the willow sticks, snipping half an inch from the bottom, and setting them back in the bucket. Each time you do this, add more water and make another batch. If it sits around too long, just toss it on the border.

Plants such as coreopsis, with netted, fibrous roots, can be gently ripped into small chunks. In all cases, any woody central bits of root should be discarded. The younger pieces should be reset in fresh soil or holding pots as quickly as you can manage. When possible, work on cool, overcast days to avoid exposing fragile roots to hot sun and drying winds. Keep a bucket of water on hand while you work. You can tuck new divisions in the water (add a handful of manure or compost to block the sun's direct rays), rinse away excess dirt, and soak dry rootballs before division.

Certain perennials, notably slow-growing variegated ones, are best increased by taking stem cuttings. Midsummer tip cuttings of fast-rooting perennials such as phlox (*Phlox paniculata*) and salvia will give you a lot of plants quickly.

■ To make stem cuttings, simply remove a few sturdy, unflowered side shoots 5 or 6 inches long and stick them, cut side down, in sandy soil.

■ For tip cuttings, take the top 3 or 4 inches of unflowered stems, choosing pieces that are flexible but substantive. Stick them, cut side down, in sandy soil. Cover the cuttings with muslin to provide shade and to conserve moisture. Most perennials will root readily without added hormones, but you can use a rooting hormone or water them daily with willow water (see above).

How to divide according to plant type

Rhizomes: *Pull or cut rhizomes apart so that each new division contains at least one bud on its rhizome. Replant each division.*

Woody roots: *A mass of crowns separates with back-to-back spading forks pushed in its center. Work them back and forth until the roots release.*

Fibrous roots: *After lifting a mature plant from the ground, use a sharp knife to split the old root system into two halves.*

PERENNIALS FOR DIFFICULT PLACES

Y ou can successfully grow perennials in nearly every gardening situation, but the key is matching the right plant to the right place. Even the most difficult "problem" areas can become beautiful opportunities, with proper selection. Use these lists as a starting point to develop your own solutions for some of the most commonly-encountered difficult areas.

TOP 10 PERENNIALS FOR WET SOILS

SUN
Marsh marigold (*Caltha palustris*)
Rose mallow (*Hibiscus moscheutos*)
Japanese iris (*Iris ensata*)
Cardinal flower (*Lobelia cardinalis*)
Yellow flag iris (*Iris pseudacorus*)

SHADE
Maidenhair fern (*Adiantum pedatum*)
Variegated Japanese sedge (*Carex morrowii* 'Variegata')
Ligularia (*Ligularia*)
Japanese primrose (*Primula japonica*)
Rodgersia (*Rodgersia pinnata*)

TOP 10 PERENNIALS FOR DRY SOILS

SUN
Butterfly weed (*Asclepias tuberosa*)
Yarrow (*Achillea*)
Blanket flower (*Gaillardia × grandiflora*)
Creeping verbena (*Verbena* hybrids)
Yucca (*Yucca filamentosa*)

SHADE
Barrenwort (*Epimedium × rubrum*)
Dwarf crested iris (*Iris cristata*)
Solomon's seal (*Polygonatum*)
Male wood fern (*Dryopteris filix-mas*)
New Zealand flax (*Phormium tenax*)

TOP 25 PERENNIALS FOR DEER RESISTANCE

SUN
Wormwood (*Artemisia ludoviciana*)
Butterfly weed (*Asclepias tuberosa*)
Globe thistle (*Echinops bannaticus*)
Spurge (*Euphorbia*)
Joe-Pye weed (*Eupatorium purpureum*)
Oriental poppy (*Papaver orientale*)
Yarrow (*Achillea*)
Monkshood (*Aconitum*)
Black-eyed Susan (*Rudbeckia fulgida*)
Yucca (*Yucca filamentosa*)
Goldenrod (*Solidago* hybrids)
Blue star (*Amsonia tabernaemontana*)
False indigo (*Baptisia australis*)

SHADE
Japanese anemone (*Anemone × hybrida*)
Goatsbeard (*Aruncus dioicus*)
Astilbe (*Astilbe*)
Japanese painted fern (*Athyrium nipponicum* 'Pictum')
Bergenia (*Bergenia cordifolia*)
Variegated Japanese sedge (*Carex morrowii* 'Variegata')
Lenten rose (*Helleborus*)
Bethlehem sage (*Pulmonaria saccharata*)
Chinese rhubarb (*Rheum palmatum*)
Bugbane (*Cimicifuga racemosa*)
Christmas fern (*Polystichum acrostichoides*)
Cinnamon fern (*Osmunda cinnamomea*)

TOP 10 PERENNIALS FOR CONTAINERS

SUN
Perennial fountain grass (*Pennisetum alopecuroides*)
Hardy chrysanthemum (*Chrysanthemum* hybrids)
Lamb's-ears (*Stachys byzantina*)
Creeping verbena (*Verbena* hybrids)
Yucca (*Yucca filamentosa*)

SHADE
Coral bells (*Heuchera* hybrids)
Astilbe (*Astilbe*)
Japanese painted fern (*Athyrium nipponicum* 'Pictum')
Bergenia (*Bergenia cordifolia*)
Variegated Japanese sedge (*Carex morrowii* 'Variegata')

TOP 10 PERENNIALS FOR SEASIDE

SUN
Wormwood (*Artemisia ludoviciana*)
Yarrow (*Achillea*)
Northern sea oats (*Chasmanthium latifolium*)
Crocosmia (*Crocosmia* hybrids)
Creeping verbena (*Verbena* hybrids)

SHADE
Japanese anemone (*Anemone × hybrida*)
Bergenia (*Bergenia cordifolia*)
Coral bells (*Heuchera* hybrids)
Beard-tongue (*Penstemon*)
New Zealand flax (*Phormium tenax*)

PERENNIAL MAINTENANCE CALENDAR

NORTHERN GARDENS

Early Spring	Late Spring	Early Summer	Late Summer	Early Fall	Late Fall	Early Winter	Late Winter
Gradually remove mulch as weather warms.	Continue weed removal, including unwanted perennials.	Weed and edge.	Weed and edge.	Weed and edge.	Weed, edge, and water, if needed.	Evaluate the year's successes and failures; plan for next year.	Order plants and seeds.
Cut back over-wintered grasses and perennials.	Mulch with a layer of organic matter to help control weeds, conserve moisture, and enrich soil.	Water, as needed.	Watering should become deeper and less frequent.	Water during dry spells.	Cut back most plants to 8 to 10".	Peruse catalogs.	Start seeds indoors.
Clear garden of dead plant material.		Fertilize.	Shear and deadhead, as needed.	Deadhead summer bloomers.	Leave certain plants for winter effects or seed heads for birds (e.g., purple coneflower, blazing star, black-eyed susan, and most grasses).	Enjoy the winter gardenscape.	Tour your garden; press in any plants that have frost-heaved.
Lift, divide, and replant crowded summer and fall bloomers.	Water new plantings, and the whole garden if less than 1" rainfall per week.	Watch for insect pests.	Lift and divide bearded irises, daylilies, and oriental poppies.	Lift and divide spring- and summer-bloomers; keep new plantings watered.		Mulch beds with old Christmas tree boughs.	Cut back plant stems that have collapsed.
Weed and edge.	Fertilize.	Shear spring bloomers for tidy appearance and to encourage rebloom.	Stake tall fall bloomers, if needed.	Prepare soil in new planting areas for spring.	Spread composted organic matter on beds.		Jot down ideas; sketch planting plans.
Add composted organic matter to beds.	Plant potted perennials.	Pinch back and thin mums and asters for fuller, bushier plants.	Cut back plants to control sprawling growth.	Finish all planting by mid-October.	Mulch after the ground freezes.		
Plant bare-root perennials.	Stake tall perennials.	Stake as needed.	Stop fertilizing.		Recyle or return used pots to accepting nurseries.		
Fertilize.	Watch for insect pests; control by hand-picking or appropriate chemicals.	Old-fashioned bleeding heart can be divided.					
Be patient with late-emerging perennials (butterfly weed, balloon flower, plumbago).	Shear or deadhead spring bloomers after they finish blooming.	Cut flowers at their prime for fresh arranging and drying.					
Sow lupine seeds where you want them to grow.	Continue dividing, as needed.						

SOUTHERN GARDENS

Early Spring	Late Spring	Early Summer	Late Summer	Early Fall	Late Fall	Early Winter	Late Winter
Control weeds before they start to spread.	Weed.	Weed.	Weed and water as needed.	Water if needed.	Clean plant debris from garden.	Planting can continue until ground freezes.	Firm in plants that have frost-heaved.
Lift, divide, and replant summer and fall bloomers.	Mulch with organic matter to control weeds, conserve moisture, and enrich soil.	Water, if needed.	Continue deadheading and light shearing as needed.	Lift and divide perennials that bloom in spring and summer.	Reduce watering.	Continue tidying up gardens.	Sow hollyhock seeds.
Plant bare-root perennials.	Water if less than 1" rainfall per week.	Keep garden well-mulched.	Plant coral bells and foxglove.	Plant violets and pinks (Dianthus) for winter bloom.	Continue to seed and plant, as desired.	Monitor weeding needs.	Plant and stake delphiniums.
Feed with high-potassium fertilizer.	Plant potted perennials.	Deadhead spent flowers regularly.	Begin direct seeding of perennials (e.g., baby's-breath, shasta daisy, and phlox).	Continue direct seeding.	Add lime to planting beds, if needed.	Mulch with composted organic matter.	Divide Christmas rose (Helleborus niger) after blooming.
Add composted organic matter to beds.	Continue staking as needed.	Shear spring bloomers for tidiness and to encourage rebloom.	Keep checking for insect pests.	Deadhead and shear foliage for tidiness.		Keep alert for frost warnings; cover plant with blankets or row covers.	Set out early spring bloomers (e.g., primroses, pinks, violas).
Protect plants from slugs and birds.	Cut back certain plants to control height (e.g. phlox and bee balm).	Lift and divide primroses and other early bloomers after they finish.		Clean beds thoroughly, removing weeds and any diseased plants.		Evaluate the year's successes and failures; plan for next year.	Order plants and seeds.
Stake plants with tall, weak stems.	Watch for insect pests; control by hand-picking or appropriate chemicals.	Stake and tie up plants as needed.				Peruse catalogs.	
Consider incorporating polymer granules into soil to increase water-holding capacity.	Continue feeding.	Continue feeding.					
		Watch for disease and promptly remove any affected plants.					
		Check for insect pests.					

PERENNIALS
SELECTION AND GROWING GUIDE

Careful selection and placement of sturdy, easy-maintenance perennials, such as Rudbeckia 'Goldsturm' and Eupatorium 'Gateway' shown here, becomes doubly important when they are massed for large-scale effect in the landscape.

Choosing a perennial is like choosing a friend: Pick carefully, and your relationship can blossom for years, enriching your life.

On the following pages, you'll find profiles of some favorite candidates for long-term happiness—many that look familiar, and some that seem exotic. Short or tall, flamboyant or subdued, our pick of the most garden-worthy perennials are here for you to look over.

Use this selection guide to learn all you can about their virtues, habits, and where they prefer to live, before you commit to a prolonged relationship. Each listing includes information you need to consider. Along with the image, you'll see a nutshell description of each perennial, as well as its traits, and the zones in which it grows best. A plant listed as suitable for zones 4 to 7 will survive winter in zones 4

and warmer, and summer in zones 7 and cooler. (See USDA Zone Map, page 92, to locate your zone.)

"Uses" gives you more information to help you decide whether you want this perennial in your garden. Here you'll find additional attributes for each perennial, along with drawbacks and a suggestion or two for other perennials that will make great partners.

"Siting and Care" describes the growing conditions necessary, such as whether the plant prefers sun or shade, wet or dry "feet," sandy or clay soil, as well as specific instructions for its planting and care.

The final section contains additional recommendations for other varieties or related species that may prove worthy of your gardening adventure.

ACHILLEA

(a-ki-LEE-uh)

Yarrow

2'

2'

- Long-lasting summer flowers
- Fernlike foliage
- Undemanding, drought resistant
- Zones 3–9

A beginning gardener's dream, yarrow is hardy throughout the country, withstanding heat, cold, and drought.

USES: Offering color in the summer garden, yarrow reblooms for weeks if old blossoms are removed.

The foliage, often silvery, complements other garden flowers. Pair with other drought-tolerant sun lovers, like false indigo (*Baptisia*) and purple coneflower (*Echinacea*).

SITING AND CARE: Best in full sun in any soil except wet clay. In rich soil, plants grow lanky and spread aggressively. Plant 2 to 3 feet apart. No need to coddle. Divide in spring every two or three years.

RECOMMENDED VARIETIES: A. *millefolium* 'Appleblossom' with lilac-pink flowers grows 2 to 3 feet tall; 'Paprika' is an intense red with yellow centers on 2-foot stems. A. 'Coronation Gold' is one of the best for drying, with prolific, 5-inch-wide golden yellow flower

heads on sturdy, 30-inch-tall stems. A. 'Moonshine' has brilliant yellow flowers and foot-tall silvery foliage.

'Coronation Gold' yarrow has broad flower heads held erect on sturdy, silvery stems.

ACONITUM

(ak-o-NYE-tum)

Monkshood

3'

1'

- Spectacular helmet-shaped flowers, summer or fall
- Glossy green leaves
- Good for cutting
- Zones 3–7 (zone 6 east of the Rocky Mountains)

Unique 1-inch flowers bloom on 3- to 4-foot plants in summer or fall, depending on variety.

USES: A good back-of-the-border plant, monkshood's blue flowers and glossy foliage blend beautifully with

other flowers. Combine with bugbane (*Cimicifuga*) or meadow rue (*Thalictrum*).

SITING AND CARE: Best in partial shade, monkshood also thrives in full sun in areas with cool summers, especially if the soil never dries out. Plant 18 inches apart in rich, fertile, well-drained soil. All parts are poisonous, so avoid planting them where children play. Avoid overwatering. Divide every three or four years. Staking may be necessary on taller varieties.

RECOMMENDED VARIETIES: A. *carmichaelii* 'Arendsii' has large blue flowers in fall. A. × *cammarum* 'Bicolor' has white hoods with a blue border. *Aconitum* 'Ivorine' is

earliest to flower, with creamy white flowers on neat, compact plants.

The stalks of Aconitum x cammarum *'Bicolor' sometimes need staking.*

ADIANTUM PEDATUM

(ad-ee-AN-tum)

Maidenhair fern

18"

18"

- Delicate and lacy
- Shiny black stems
- Light green fronds
- Zones 3–8

One of the most beautiful and refined ferns, maidenhair grows 10 to 24 inches tall, with an 18-inch spread. Fronds grow in an unusual "five-finger" pattern.

USES: This elegant fern is gorgeous in moist woodland gardens and as a filler in bouquets. It looks magnificent when paired with

Solomon's seal (*Polygonatum*) or hosta.

SITING AND CARE: Plant ferns 18 inches apart in filtered light, protected from direct sun. Performs best in moist, neutral to limey soil enriched with organic matter. Add agricultural lime to acid soils. Make sure to water regularly during dry summer months.

RECOMMENDED VARIETIES: 'Japonicum' has fronds which emerge a pinkish bronze color. 'Miss Sharples' has larger leaflets and chartreuse new growth. A. *venustum* is 12 inches tall with pale green fronds on purplish black stems. Fronds have a blue tint in summer, and turn yellow-brown in autumn.

Adiantum pedatum is unmatched for graceful foliage in moist shade.

AGASTACHE FOENICULUM

(ag-uh-STAY-kee)

Anise hyssop

The five-inch flower spikes of 'Fragrant Delight' anise hyssop top erect, 3-foot plants in late summer.

30"
30"

- Bold late-summer flower clusters
- Fragrant leaves
- Attracts hummingbirds
- Zones 6–9

A vertical plant twice as tall as it is wide, anise hyssop makes a good substitute for invasive loosestrife.
USES: This late-blooming perennial adds a boldness to the border at summer's end. Its leaves are useful for tea or seasoning; its flowers are favored for drying. It also attracts bees and butterflies. Pair with beebalm (*Monarda*) or with any late-summer yellow flowers, like goldenrod (*Solidago*).

SITING AND CARE: Prefers moist, well-drained soil and full sun but tolerates light shade. Easy to grow from seeds or nursery plants. Space 18 inches apart. Thin volunteer plants and remove spent flowers. Can be aggressive.
RECOMMENDED VARIETIES AND RELATED SPECIES:
'Fragrant Delight' has stiff spikes of pale blue flowers on 3-foot-tall stems. 'Snow Spike' forms a bushy plant with white flower spikes. *A. rupestris*, native to the southwestern U.S., is a hardy, attractive wildflower with rosy orange flowers and gray-green fragrant foliage. *A. barberi* 'Tutti Frutti' has tubular pink flowers from midsummer to frost.

ALCEA ROSEA

(al-SEE-uh)

Hollyhock

Hollyhock's spikes of cup-shaped flowers top tall, coarse-leaved plants.

5'
2'

- Towering mid-summer flower spikes
- Old-fashioned favorite
- Attracts butterflies
- Zones 3–7

Short-lived and often considered a biennial, hollyhock is a must for the cottage garden. The plant grows 5 to 8 feet tall or more.
USES: Great for vertical effect or a living screen, hollyhock is prized for its old-fashioned charm. Combine with old-fashioned, daisylike sun lovers, like Helen's flower (*Helenium*) or black-eyed Susan (*Rudbeckia*). Although short-lived, the plant self-seeds. Not for the

finicky gardener, hollyhock often suffers from leaf spot, rust, slugs, and Japanese beetles.
SITING AND CARE: This back-of-the-border plant is ideal for full sun and rich, moist, well-drained soil. Easy from seed. Space transplants or seeds 12 inches apart. Be sure to remove diseased foliage as soon as it appears and, if necessary, spray with fungicide to control rust.
RECOMMENDED VARIETIES:
'Chater's Double' has double flowers in maroon, red, rose, white, and yellow. 'Nigra' is wine-purple, earning it the name "black" hollyhock. 'Indian Spring' is a single, available in white, yellow, rose, and pink, 7 to 8 feet tall.

A great ground cover for light shade, lady's mantle looks like green foam when planted under trees or shrubs.

ALCHEMILLA MOLLIS

(al-kuh-MILL-uh)

Lady's mantle

1'
2'

- Frothy flowers, late spring or early summer
- Scalloped, fan-shaped leaves
- Easy to grow
- Zones 4–7

Tiny chartreuse flowers arch from foot-tall mounds of marvelous, cup-shaped gray-green leaves that resemble a woman's cloak.
USES: Quick to spread, lady's mantle makes an ideal ground cover. Although lady's mantle is

grown primarily for its unique, dew-catching leaves, its dainty flowers are favorites for cutting or drying. Combines well with either bergenia or wood fern (*Dryopteris*).
SITING AND CARE: Plant in partial shade, or in full sun in cool northern areas. Moist but well-drained soil of average fertility is ideal. Space plants 10 inches apart in clumps of three or more. Cut back foliage in midsummer if leaves look ragged. Division is seldom necessary. Be sure to remove spent flowers if plants become invasive.
RELATED SPECIES: Alpine lady's mantle (*A. alpina*) stands only 6 inches tall, has deeply cut leaves edged with silver, and a tidy habit.

AMSONIA TABERNAEMONTANA

(am-SOH-nee-uh)

Blue star

3'
- Clusters of blue starlike flowers in spring
- Willowlike foliage turns gold in fall
- Easy to grow
- Zones 3–9

Resembling a 2-foot-tall willow tree, native blue star is basically long-lived and maintenance free. It is one of the best perennials for reliable fall foliage color.

USES: Effective in masses, the soft, willowlike texture contrasts effectively with other garden plants. Never invasive, this care-free plant grows slowly and looks beautiful paired with bergenia or cushion spurge (*Euphorbia*), and makes a lovely companion for peonies.

SITING AND CARE: Plant in partial shade or full sun, in virtually any soil, moist or dry. Set nursery plants 12 inches apart. Division is seldom necessary, and pests and diseases are not a problem. Shear back to 6 inches after flowering to keep plants from getting too tall.

RELATED SPECIES: Arkansas amsonia (*A. hubrectii*) has lacy foliage, steel blue flowers and brilliant yellow fall foliage color.

Blue star's late spring flowers (above) and bright green leaves are followed by gold autumn foliage (right).

ANEMONE X HYBRIDA

(uh-NEM-oh-nee)

Japanese anemone

3'
- Silky flowers, late summer into fall
- Superior cut flowers
- Lush, maplelike leaves
- Zones 5–8 (zone 7 east of the Rocky Mountains)

The silky sheen of 2- to 3-inch pink or white flowers perks up the late-summer garden.

USES: Excellent for the middle border, anemone hybrids bear clusters of 10 or more flowers on plants that grow 2 to 5 feet tall and wide. Attractive foliage. Stunning when combined with Japanese painted fern (*Athyrium*).

SITING AND CARE: Plant 18 inches apart in partial shade (full sun in cool climates) and rich, moist soil. Protect from wind. In order to survive harsh winters, good drainage is a must. In zones 5 and 6, plants benefit from a loose winter mulch, such as evergreen boughs. Shoots are slow to emerge in spring. Division is rarely required.

RECOMMENDED VARIETIES AND RELATED SPECIES: 'Honorine Jobert' is 3 feet tall and the hardiest white. *A. tomentosa* 'Robustissima' is hardy to zone 4.

Pasque flower (*Pulsatilla vulgaris*) is suited to alpine settings, and wood anemone (*A. nemorosa*) naturalizes in shady woodland locations.

Graceful pink 'September Charm' arises from dark green foliage.

AQUILEGIA

(ak-wi-LEE-jee-uh)

Columbine

2'
- Curious, spurred spring flowers
- Wide color range
- Hummingbird favorite
- Zones 3–9

Columbine, with blue, pink, red, white, or yellow flowers, grows to heights from 6 inches to 3 feet.

USES: Long lasting as cut flowers, columbine naturalizes in semi-shaded woodland gardens. Use with hydrangeas or white wood aster (*Aster divaricatus*). Use dwarf varieties in the rock garden. Often short-lived but readily self-sows.

SITING AND CARE: Plant 1 to 2 feet apart, depending on variety, in well-drained soil in partial shade. Or sow seeds in spring for flowers the following year. Keep soil moist. Remove and destroy leaves disfigured by leaf miners.

RECOMMENDED VARIETIES AND RELATED SPECIES: Canada columbine (*A. canadensis*), a native wildflower with red spurs and yellow sepals, makes a dependable naturalizer. A. 'McKanna Hybrids Improved' is a large-flowered hybrid with bicolored blossoms. 'Ministar' (*A. flabellata*) has bright blue and white flowers on dwarf, 6-inch-tall plants. *A. chrysantha* has long-spurred yellow flowers and a long period of bloom.

'Nora Barlow' is an unusual columbine with full, double flowers.

ARTEMISIA LUDOVICIANA

(ar-teh-MISS-ee-uh)

Wormwood

- Frosty silver foliage
- Aromatic
- Drought tolerant
- Zones 4–9

Silvery-gray 'Powis Castle' foliage makes a pretty foil for other flowers.

A fine, easy-to-grow foliage plant, wormwood forms spreading clumps 2 to 3 feet tall, but may decline in warmer areas with high humidity.
USES: Thriving in poor soil and drought, wormwood provides excellent contrast of color and texture. Perfect for drought-tolerant gardens, paired with tall stonecrop (*Sedum* 'Autumn Joy') or with black-eyed Susan (*Rudbeckia fulgida* 'Goldsturm'). Prized for dried-flower arrangements.
SITING AND CARE: Full sun and well-drained soil are the only requirements. Plant 2 feet apart. Don't fertilize or overwater. Divide often to curtail aggressive growth, especially in sandy, southern areas.
RECOMMENDED VARIETIES AND RELATED SPECIES: 'Valerie Finnis' is 18 to 24 inches tall, with wide, felty leaves, does well in cool climates. *A. arborescens* 'Powis Castle' forms dense mounds of lacy foliage to 3 feet, and is the best choice for the South. *A.* 'Huntington Garden' is a 4-foot-tall form with finely divided silver leaves persisting into winter. *A. stelleriana* 'Boughton Silver' is 2 feet tall with deeply toothed leaves.

ARUNCUS DIOICUS

(uh-RUN-kus)

Goatsbeard

- Showy, creamy mid-summer plumes
- Shrublike
- Attractive foliage
- Zones 3–8 (zone 7 east of the Rocky Mountains)

Goatsbeard's graceful plumes show off over its shrublike mass.

A stately perennial for light shade, goatsbeard resembles astilbe.
USES: A dramatic, large plant for back of the border or for a shrublike accent, its light green foliage is attractive all season. Needs plenty of space but makes a striking cloud of white blossoms. Combines especially well with astilbe or queen-of-the-prairie (*Filipendula*).
SITING AND CARE: Best in humus-rich, moist soil under a high tree canopy. Appreciates a little afternoon shade, and moisture is necessary for flowering in the South. Space 3 to 5 feet apart. Water generously and deeply (to avoid brown and crispy leaves) and fertilize during the growing season. Long-lived and noninvasive, goatsbeard has no serious pests and needs no staking, despite its impressive height. Division of this streamside perennial is seldom necessary and can be quite difficult.
RECOMMENDED VARIETIES AND RELATED SPECIES: 'Kneiffii' matures at 3 feet, perfect for small gardens. *A. aethusifolius* is a dwarf form (12 inches) good for small gardens, with lacy foliage.

ASCLEPIAS TUBEROSA

(a-SKLEE-pee-us)

Butterfly weed

- Brilliant flower clusters, late spring, early summer
- Attracts monarchs
- Drought tolerant
- Zones 4–9

Butterfly weed's large clusters of orange-red flowers are so vibrant, they seem to jump out at you.

A native prairie plant, 2 to 3 feet tall, butterfly weed is highly ornamental, blooms in vibrant colors, and tolerates seaside conditions.
USES: A must for the butterfly garden. Butterfly weed is a good choice for a meadow garden because it can compete successfully with grasses. Or use in a hot-colored border, combined with yarrow (*Achillea*). Its flowers are excellent for cutting, seedpods for dried flower arrangements.
SITING AND CARE: Plant 12 to 18 inches apart, in full sun in lean to average, light, well-drained soil. May also sow seeds in spring. Requires no division. Plants are slow to emerge in late spring, so be sure to mark location. Mature plants don't transplant well.
RECOMMENDED VARIETIES AND RELATED SPECIES: 'Gay Butterflies' is a showy mix of yellow, red, and orange flowers. Swamp milkweed (*A. incarnata*) has pink flowers on 3- to 4-foot, moisture-loving plants. *A. incarnata* 'Ice Ballet' has persistent ivory-white flowers on 3- to 5-foot stems.

ASTER

(ASS-ter)

Hardy aster

3'
- Early summer to late fall flowers, depending on variety
3'
- Wide color range
- Native wildflower
- Zones 4–9

From 9-inch spreading varieties to 6-foot giants, asters come in blue, crimson, pink, purple, red, or white. Many varieties may be short-lived in the deep South.
USES: Aster is an excellent fall color alternative to chrysanthemums. Taller varieties are a good choice for a meadow garden.
SITING AND CARE: Plant 12 to 20 inches apart in full sun in most regions, partial shade in the South. It's not picky about soil, but light, moist, well-drained soil of average fertility is best. Pinch in late spring to produce dense plants. Taller varieties will need staking. Divide every other year. Good air circulation and adequate moisture help control mildew.
RECOMMENDED VARIETIES AND RELATED SPECIES: *A. novae-angliae* 'Alma Potschke' is brilliant pink, 3 to 4 feet tall, and mildew resistant. *A. × frikartii* 'Monch', 2 feet tall, produces masses of lovely blue flowers from midsummer on. White wood aster (*A. divaricatus*), 1 to 2 feet tall, is the most shade tolerant.

Aster 'Monch' attracts butterflies and makes an excellent cut flower.

ASTILBE

(uh-STILL-bee)

Astilbe

3'
- Fluffy plumes, late spring and early summer
- Favorite for shade
- Attractive, ferny foliage
2'
- Zones 4–8

Feathery, long-lasting flowers of lavender, pink, red, or white bloom on 1- to 3-foot-tall plants.
Uses: A surefire way to brighten the shady garden, astilbe is showy, long-lived, and easy to grow. Superb for the woodland border or in masses for a ground cover. The plumes are good for cutting and drying.
SITING AND CARE: Plant 1 to 2 feet apart in partial shade in fertile, well-drained soil. Fertilize in spring and water well. Divide every three or four years for best performance.
RECOMMENDED VARIETIES AND RELATED SPECIES: *A. × arendsii* 'Bridal Veil' is 2 to 3 feet tall with pinkish white flowers; 'Fanal' is 2 feet tall, early to flower, with dark red flowers above bronze leaves; 'Rheinland' has clear pink flowers on 24-inch-tall plants. *A. chinensis* 'Pumila' is a dwarf form with pinkish violet blossoms under a foot tall. Its late-summer bloom and tolerance of dry conditions make it very useful. *A. simplicifolia* 'Sprite' has soft pink plumes on 12-inch plants.

Astilbe is a popular and excellent plant for shady, moist conditions.

ASTRANTIA MAJOR

(a-STRAN-shi-uh)

Masterwort

30"
- Attractive late-spring flower clusters
18"
- Bold, cutleaf clumps
- Outstanding in shade
- Zones 5–7

A charming and interesting cottage garden flower, masterwort grows 2 to 3 feet tall in cool climates but struggles in the South. White, rose, and pink flowers can all occur in the same planting over the years.
USES: Its blossoms add interesting texture to shady borders and to bouquets, and are excellent for cutting and drying. Dynamite combined with a pink variety of astilbe or with hosta.
SITING AND CARE: Thrives in shade or part shade. Needs moist but well-drained soil of average fertility. Plant 12 to 18 inches apart. Water to keep soil moist. Pests and diseases are seldom a problem, but reseeding sometimes can be. Division is not required.
RECOMMENDED VARIETIES: 'Alba' produces 2-foot white flowers over a long period. 'Lars' is a vigorous variety with dark red flowers. 'Prima Donna' produces blossoms in shades of purple on 30-inch-tall plants.

'Ruby Wedding' is a deep-red selection of masterwort.

ATHYRIUM NIPPONICUM 'PICTUM'

(a-THEER-ee-um)

Japanese painted fern

- Beautiful accent plant
- Good perennial partner
- Exquisite coloring
- Zones 3–8

Silver markings and wine-red stems highlight the Japanese painted fern.

Easy-to-grow lady fern is an excellent choice for new gardeners.

This small, 12- to 18-inch fern looks like it was painted with muted colors, and it is quite easy to grow.
USES: The most colorful of garden ferns, Japanese painted fern pairs well with primrose (*Primula*) or dwarf astilbe.
SITING AND CARE: Thrives in full shade but develops its best color in filtered light. Requires moist, well-drained, humus-rich soil. Plant a foot apart for colorful ground cover, 2 feet apart for accent. Don't allow soil to dry out.
RELATED SPECIES: Graceful lady fern (*A. filix-femina*) is vigorous and tall (up to 3 feet) but looks lacy and delicate. Tolerant of dry soil and easy to grow.

AURINIA SAXATILIS

(oh-RIN-ee-uh)

Basket-of-gold

- Brilliant yellow spring blossoms
- Gray-green foliage
- Makes a low mat
- Zones 3–7

Tiny yellow flowers completely cover 10-inch, bushy plants. Basket-of-gold struggles in hot, humid areas and is often short-lived.
USES: Ideal for dry, poor soil, basket-of-gold is useful in front of borders or in rock gardens and is especially attractive spilling over

Canary yellow flowers of basket-of-gold stand out from a distance.

rock walls. Pairs excellently with *Verbena* 'Homestead Purple' or *Phlox divaricata* 'Louisiana'.
SITING AND CARE: Plant in a sunny area with excellent drainage. Plant 8 to 12 inches apart. Should be cut back after flowering. Water only in drought and don't fertilize. Division in the fall is the easiest method of propagation.
RECOMMENDED VARIETIES: 'Citrina' is 10 to 15 inches tall with lemon yellow flowers. 'Dudley Neville' grows to 10 inches tall and has buff-colored flowers; there is also a variegated version called 'Dudley Neville Variegated'. 'Tom Thumb' is only 3 to 6 inches tall, but a vigorous selection.

BAPTISIA AUSTRALIS

(bap-TISS-ee-uh)

False indigo

- Showy indigo blue spring flowers
- Shrubby habit
- Attractive black pods
- Zones 3–8

A reliable, easy-to-grow, and long-lived North American native, false indigo stands 3 or 4 feet tall and spreads equally wide.
USES: Attractive flowers give way to decorative seedpods, which look great in dried arrangements. This shrublike plant is useful as the backbone of the border or as a living screen, and its attractive foliage lasts all season. Its drought tolerance makes it a good candidate for the wildflower meadow. Use it as

Twelve-inch spikes of pea-shaped flowers complement the lush, blue-green foliage of false indigo.

a background for coreopsis.
SITING AND CARE: Best in full sun. Sturdy plants need no staking. Plant 3 feet apart in well-drained, neutral or acid soil of average fertility. New shoots resemble dark shoots of asparagus. Water in dry weather until established. Remove spent flowers to prolong bloom. Taproot makes division or transplanting unlikely to succeed. No serious problems.
RELATED SPECIES: *B. alba*, white wild indigo, grows 2 to 3 feet tall with a 3-foot spread. A later bloomer, it does well in partial shade. *B. pendula* is very similar to *B. alba* but smaller with a more drooping growth habit.

BERGENIA CORDIFOLIA

(ber-GEE-nee-uh)

Bergenia

1'

- Springtime flower clusters
- Bold, shiny leaves
- Ground cover in shady spots

1'

- Zones 4–8 (zone 7 east of the Rocky Mountains)

This foot-tall evergreen plant spreads slowly by rhizomes and is ideal for ground cover under trees. Cabbagelike bergenia does not tolerate excessive drought or heat.

USES: Bergenia is grown primarily for showy foliage which turns bronze-red in winter unless temperatures are harsh. Irregular flower clusters are held above leaves on thick stalks, blooming pink, purple, red, or white. Nice with bleeding heart (*Dicentra*) or ferns.

SITING AND CARE: Plant 12 to 18 inches apart in shade, particularly in areas with hot summers. Bergenia performs well in almost any rich, moist, well-drained soil. Limit water and fertilizer to control spreading. Control slugs. Divide if crowded.

RECOMMENDED VARIETIES: 'Bressingham White' starts out pink and gradually turns pure white. 'Bressingham Ruby' has bright pink flowers and outstanding, deep red fall foliage. 'Perfect' has large round leaves and deep pink flowers on 18-inch stems.

Bergenia *'Bressingham Ruby'* bears deep pink flowers in early spring.

BOLTONIA ASTEROIDES

(bowl-TOH-nee-uh)

Boltonia

5'

- Spectacular plant
- Profuse daisylike flowers in fall
- Tall, strong stemmed
- Zones 4–8

3'

Native to open woodlands of eastern North America, boltonia seldom needs staking despite its impressive 4- or 5-foot height.

USES: With its 1-inch daisies, white and pink with yellow centers, boltonia looks like an aster. Plant in combination with Japanese anemone, ornamental grasses, or Russian sage (*Perovskia*).

SITING AND CARE: Plant 18 inches apart in full sun or partial shade. In the South, shade is preferred, but staking may be required (may be too floppy for the formal garden). Thrives in any soil, but well-drained soil of average fertility is best. Cut back to 12 inches in late spring if needed to control height. Divide every three or four years. Resistant to mildew.

RECOMMENDED VARIETIES: 'Pink Beauty' sports lavender-pink blossoms with silver-blue foliage. 'Snowbank' has extra-sturdy stems, vertical habit, snowy white flowers, and blue-green leaves.

Clouds of flowers completely cover Boltonia 'Snowbank' in autumn.

CALAMAGROSTIS X ACUTIFLORA 'STRICTA'

(kal-a-ma-GROSS-tis)

Feather reed grass

4'

- Early flowering (June)
- Upright, erect habit
- Easy and adaptable
- Zones 6–9

2'

Vase-shaped, 5- to 7-foot-tall clumps offer strong vertical effect and tolerate seaside conditions.

USES: This is one of the few grasses that will thrive in wet clay. Group with black-eyed Susan (*Rudbeckia*) or stonecrop (Sedum 'Autumn Joy') for beauty that lasts well into the winter months.

SITING AND CARE: Plant 2 feet apart in full sun in ordinary or moist soil. Divide crowded clumps in spring after new growth begins.

RECOMMENDED VARIETIES: 'Karl Foerster' blooms 2 weeks earlier than 'Stricta' and is slightly shorter. 'Overdam' is a variegated dwarf form with 12- to 18-inch mounds of white-striped foliage.

The feathery plumes of feather reed grass turn a soft wheat color in midsummer. It makes a strong vertical element, and an elegant gauzy screen.

Full sun is necessary for marsh marigold's best performance.

CALTHA PALUSTRIS

(KAL-tha)

Marsh marigold

15"

15"

- Bright yellow spring blossoms
- Handsome foliage
- Great for bog gardens
- Zones 5–7 (Zone 6 east of the Rocky Mountains)

This wetland native forms attractive foot-tall clumps of rounded, kidney-shaped leaves (which get smaller as they progress up the stem) topped with 1- to 2-inch yellow flowers. Marsh marigold often goes dormant after flowering.

USES: Ideal for low-lying spots where water stands. Match with water iris or pickerel weed.
SITING AND CARE: Plant in full sun or partial shade in a bog, water garden, or in a running stream. Plant 18 inches apart in wet soil or submerge crown 1 inch in water garden. If crowded, divide during summer dormancy.
RECOMMENDED VARIETIES: 'Flore Plena' ('Multiplex') is an outstanding showy double form with 2-inch-wide yellow flowers. 'Alba' has brilliant white flowers which contrast strikingly with the shiny foliage, but it is much more difficult to obtain.

CAMPANULA PERSICIFOLIA

(kam-PAN-yew-la)

Peach-leaf bellflower

Sprays of dainty blue or white bells are held high above strap-shaped leaves of peach-leaf bellflower.

2'

2'

- Bell-shaped flowers, early to midsummer
- Exceptional for cutting
- Very easy to grow
- Zones 3–7

Appealing 1½-inch flowers, which almost resemble a saucer, bloom on plants 2 or 3 feet tall. One of the best bellflowers for the South.
USES: A favorite for long-lasting cut flowers, this plant reblooms if deadheaded. Lovely in combination with foxglove (*Digitalis*).
SITING AND CARE: Plant in sun or partial shade in neutral or alkaline soil that is rich and well-drained. Space plants 12 to 18 inches apart. Water as needed to prevent wilting. Overwatering encourages crown rot. Remove spent blossoms. Divide when crowding causes clumps to decline.
RELATED SPECIES: Carpathian bellflower (*C. carpatica*) is popular and a petite 6 to 9 inches tall, with 1-inch, violet-blue bells. Makes an ideal rock garden plant and tolerates a wide range of conditions. Milky bellflower (*C. lactiflora*) has a bushy habit and grows 3 to 5 feet tall. Canterbury bells (*C. medium*) is an old-fashioned favorite biennial. Serbian bellflower (*C. poscharskyana*), with pale blue, starry flowers, makes a good rock garden specimen or ground cover.

The striped leaves of variegated Japanese sedge appear to swirl.

CAREX MORROWII 'VARIEGATA'

(KARE-eks)

Variegated Japanese sedge

1'

1'

- Low, arching form
- For sun or shade
- Undemanding
- Zones 5–9

The silvery white-margined foliage is evergreen in the South; semi-evergreen in the North.
USES: This compact grass look-alike is an excellent choice for shady borders, and in Southern gardens will supply year-round beauty and interest. It is pretty as an accent, in masses, or as an edging. Dense growth continues to become denser with time.
SITING AND CARE: Plant in full or partial shade in the South, sun in the North. Prefers a moist, well-drained soil. Space 18 inches apart. Don't overwater. Cut back previous year's foliage in the spring.
RELATED SPECIES: *C. elata* 'Bowles Golden' is 24 inches tall and terrifically handsome. Its bright golden yellow leaves with thin green margins show well in the shade. The yellow color fades as summer temperatures rise.

CENTRANTHUS RUBER

(ken-TRAN-thus)

Red valerian

2'
■ Iridescent reddish-pink blooms all summer
■ Drought tolerant
2' ■ Easy to grow
■ Zones 5–8 (zone 4 with protection)

This old-fashioned, bushy plant (also known as Jupiter's beard) grows to 2 feet in mild climates but can't take the combined heat and humidity of the Deep South.
USES: Easy-to-grow red valerian is one of the longest-blooming perennials. Its numerous flowers are especially beautiful combined with wormwood (*Artemesia*) or lamb's-ears (*Stachys*).

SITING AND CARE: Plant 12 to 15 inches apart in full sun in well-drained, neutral to alkaline soil. Performs well in stone walls. Deadhead to promote repeat blooms. Division isn't necessary for this short-lived perennial. Pests are never a problem. Division in the spring or fall is needed to maintain its true colors.
RECOMMENDED VARIETIES: 'Albus' produces ivory-white flowers and is an excellent variety. 'Coccineus' is a variety with deep rose-red blossoms.

Red valerian's showy flowers contrast with gray-green leaves.

CERATOSTIGMA PLUMBAGINOIDES

(ser-a-toh-STIG-ma)

Plumbago

8"
■ Intense blue flowers, late summer to fall
15" ■ Glossy-green leaves turn bronze in fall
■ Good ground cover
■ Zones 5 to 9

This slow and low (8- to 12-inch) grower spreads by underground stems and is perfect for rocky areas.
USES: Masses of gentian blue flowers from summer to late fall plus red-tinged leaves in autumn add long-lasting seasonal color. Underplant spring-blooming bulbs for all-season interest. Use as a ground cover in sunny spots or allow it to ramble over small rocks.
SITING AND CARE: Prefers well-drained soil in sun or partial shade. Space 12 inches apart. In areas where tops aren't killed by cold, cut back hard in early spring. Divide in early spring if clumps die out in center. Late to emerge in spring.
RELATED SPECIES: Griffith's leadwort (*C. griffithii*) is a similarly handsome plant with deep blue flowers, with the addition of red-margined foliage that is evergreen. It is hardy in zones 6 to 8.

Plumbago is a low-growing spreader with blue flowers and red fall foliage.

CHASMANTHIUM LATIFOLIUM

(kas-MAN-thee-um)

Northern sea oats

30"
■ Pretty in 3 seasons
■ Useful in dried arrangements
18" ■ Bronze fall color
■ Zones 3–8

Flower stems arch from light green, 3-foot-tall bamboolike clumps. This grass may self-seed.
USES: One of the best grasses for partial shade. Its flowers are lovely in dried arrangements and as a focal point or ground cover in the garden.

SITING AND CARE: Plant in sun or partial shade in rich, well-drained soil. Space 24 inches apart.

The grainlike flowers of sea oats wave in the breeze on wiry stems.

Northern sea oats starts green and turns bronze as fall approaches.

CHRYSANTHEMUM HYBRIDS

(kri-SAN-theh-mum)

Hardy chrysanthemums are excellent choices for beds of fall flower color.

Hardy chrysanthemum

- Exquisite show autumn to frost, depending on variety
- Huge choice of colors, shapes
- Easily transplanted in bloom
- Zones 5–9

One of the oldest cultivated plants, "mums" bloom in just about every choice of color except blue, from simple single flowers to highly complex, decorative doubles on 1- to 3-foot-tall plants.

USES: These are not the fall mums of the discount store (which are also hardy and sometimes sold as Korean mums). Chrysanthemums offer unsurpassed fall color, and are especially effective massed in beds.

SITING AND CARE: Well-drained soil is a must, particularly for winter survival. Plant in full sun. Space plants 18 to 24 inches apart. Provide ample water and fertilizer throughout summer. Pinch tip growth several times before mid-summer to produce bushier plants. Control spider mites or aphids with insecticidal soap spray. Remove and destroy plants with aster yellows, a disease which inhibits growth. Be sure to stake taller varieties. Mulch after the ground freezes.

Also known as black snakeroot, bugbane blooms in the shady border.

CIMICIFUGA RACEMOSA

(si-mi-si-FEW-ga)

Bugbane

- Graceful midsummer ivory spikes
- Statuesque
- Long-lived native
- Zones 3–7

Eight-inch, long-stemmed flower spikes top a 4- to 6-foot clump.

USES: A must for the shade garden. Perfect for the back of a border or with other shade lovers such as Solomon's seal (*Polygonatum*) and hostas.

SITING AND CARE: Plant in filtered shade in soil that is deep, rich, moist, and well-drained. Space nursery plants 3 feet apart. In warm areas, mulch to keep soil cool and moist. Water and fertilize regularly. Clumps rarely need division. Be patient: they often require a few years before putting on a show.

RECOMMENDED VARIETIES: *C. japonica* stands 3 feet tall, with erect white spikes late summer to early fall. *C. ramosa atropurpurea* (purple-branched bugbane) is 4 to 6 feet tall, an elegant plant with purple-flushed leaves and creamy white flowers. *C. simplex* 'White Pearl' blooms in autumn with eye-catching 3-foot-tall white spikes; the best species for the South.

COREOPSIS VERTICILLATA

(kore-ee-OP-sis)

Threadleaf Coreopsis

'Moonbeam' coreopsis bears pale yellow flowers all summer.

- Blooms all summer
- Fine-textured leaves
- Drought resistant
- Zones 5–9

Free-flowering, 1½- to 2-inch yellow blossoms are held on 18- to 24-inch stalks.

USES: This easy-to-grow plant stages a long-lasting flower show that's not to be missed. Beautiful with any blue or purple flowers, such as perennial salvia or balloon flower (*Platycodon*).

SITING AND CARE: Plant in sunny spot in soil of average fertility. Space 18 inches apart. After the first flush of summer blossoms, cut off the flowers, and an autumn rebloom will follow. Divide if flowering declines.

RECOMMENDED VARIETIES AND RELATED SPECIES: 'Moonbeam' is a standout (and the most popular variety), with loads of pale yellow flowers. 'Zagreb' has deep yellow flowers. *C. grandiflora* 'Early Sunrise' produces 2-inch, semidouble, golden yellow flowers; 'Flying Saucers' is a new variety with a compact habit, 15 inches tall, and single gold flowers produced June until frost. Pink threadleaf coreopsis (*C. rosea*) has wonderful 1-inch-wide, pink flowers on erect, delicate stems with lacy foliage; best for cooler climates.

CORTADERIA SELLOANA

(kor-ta-DER-ee-uh)

Pampas grass

7'
5'
- Majestic feathery plumes late summer through winter
- Fountain shape
- Useful in dried arrangements
- Zones 6–9

Standing 6 to 15 feet tall with a spread of 5 or 6 feet, it's the largest and showiest of the grasses. In colder zones, grow in a container and winter in the greenhouse.
USES: Pampas grass is a most dramatic accent and looks best as a focal point, planted with an unobstructed background. For the showiest plumes, be sure to purchase a female plant. Flower color varies from silver to creamy white.
SITING AND CARE: Plant in full sun in moist, well-drained soil. Water and fertilize regularly. Before new growth begins in spring, cut back and remove dead material collected near base.
RECOMMENDED VARIETIES: 'Andes Silver' is 6 to 7 feet tall with large silvery flower plumes. 'Pumila' is a dwarf with creamy white flowers on 3- to 4-foot stalks. Very floriferous. 'Patagonia' is 5 to 6 feet tall with striking bluish foliage.

Magnificent feathery plumes of pampas grass last through winter.

CORYDALIS LUTEA

(koh-RID-uh-lis)

Yellow corydalis

12"
18"
- Fragrant yellow flowers, spring and intermittently in summer
- Ferny foliage
- Low, mounding form
- Zones 5–7

Low mounds of blue-green foliage, 12 to 15 inches tall. Self-sows and can naturalize in shady gardens; goes dormant and often disappears in hot weather.
USES: Small but showy, corydalis is ideal to tuck into tiny spaces in the shady border. An elegant filler, it does well on walls, and planted in cracks in paving. Nice for the front of the border with small hostas.
SITING AND CARE: Plant young nursery plants a foot apart in partial shade in rich, moist, well-drained soil. Deadhead to promote rebloom. Don't disturb difficult-to-transplant mature plants. Normally no pests or diseases bother this plant.
RECOMMENDED VARIETIES AND RELATED SPECIES: Blue corydalis (*C. flexuosa*) 'Blue Panda' has sky blue flowers and grows 12 to 15 inches tall. White corydalis (*C. ochroleuca*) has ivory flowers above appealing blue-gray foliage.

Clusters of yellow corydalis (above) show off; blue corydalis (right) does well in cooler climates.

CROCOSMIA HYBRIDS

(kroh-KOZ-mee-uh)

Crocosmia

2'
1'
- Brilliant color, mid to late summer
- Excellent cut flower
- Attracts hummingbirds
- Zones 5–8

Crocosmia, also known as montbretia, has orange, scarlet, or yellow flowers, which stand 18 to 40 inches tall amid swordlike leaves. Its corms should be lifted in fall in northern gardens and overwintered.
USES: Crocosmia is unsurpassed for midseason color and for long-lasting cut flowers. Looks great combined with ornamental grasses.
SITING AND CARE: Plant in well-drained soil, in full sun in the North, partial shade in the South. Space nursery plants 6 to 8 inches apart or plant corms 2 or 3 inches deep. Divide every three years to increase flowering. Control spider mites with insecticidal soap spray.
RECOMMENDED VARIETIES: C. 'Lucifer' is exceptional and covered with 36-inch-tall scarlet-red flowers. C. × *crocosmiiflora* 'Citronella' has small lemon yellow flowers; impressive 'Emily McKenzie' has vibrant orange flowers with crimson throats.

Flaming red wands of Crocosmia 'Lucifer' rise above iris-like leaves.

DELPHINIUM X ELATUM

(del-FIN-ee-um)

Delphinium

Tall spires of blue delphinium begin their annual display in June.

- ■ Tall, bold, rich blue spikes bloom in spring
- ■ Repeat blooms
- ■ Good for cutting
- ■ Zones 2–7

Although famous for its blue flowers, delphinium also comes in pink, purple, red, violet, and white. This columnar plant reaches 4 to 6 feet.
USES: Short-lived and prone to disease, this statuesque plant is worth the effort. Try blue delphium with threadleaf coreopsis (*Coreopsis* 'Moonbeam') and yarrow (*Achillea*) for a winning combination.
SITING AND CARE: Plant in a protected spot in full sun in rich, moist, well-drained soil that is neutral or slightly alkaline. Space plants 2 or 4 feet apart. Stake. If necessary, use fungicides to control mildew and other diseases. Cutting old flower stems to the ground encourages repeat blooms.

RECOMMENDED VARIETIES AND RELATED SPECIES: Cultivars include Pacific Hybrids, which boast showy spikes of clear, brightly colored double flowers. Magic Fountains cultivars produce 2½- to 3-foot-tall bushy plants and come in a range of colors, many with dark centers. Hardier than taller types. Belladonna delphinium (*D. × belladonna*) has loose, multiple stalks and performs better in hot areas than other delphiniums.

Graceful, tapering fronds of hay-scented fern form attractive clumps.

DENNSTAEDTIA PUNCTILOBULA

(den-STET-ee-uh)

Hay-scented fern

- ■ Adaptable
- ■ Lacy texture
- ■ Spreads by rhizomes
- ■ Zones 3–8 (zone 7 east of the Rocky Mountains)

The dried or crushed yellow-green fronds of this North American native fern smell like crushed hay. Beautiful, hairy, arching fronds grow 2 to 3 feet tall.
USES: This easy-to-grow fern tolerates a wide range of conditions. Use it to provide ground cover in a shady border. A beautiful backdrop for Japanese anemone or bugbane (*Cimicifuga*). Slugs and snails may be a problem. In the autumn its fronds turn a soft yellow color.
SITING AND CARE: Grows best in partial to deep shade in rich, moist, well-drained, acid soil but will tolerate open sun and a wide range of soil conditions. Once established, it can survive in fairly dry soil. Plant 3 feet apart. May become too invasive for the small garden but is attractive and care-free in large gardens where it has room to roam. Pairs beautifully with large boulders.

Deschampsia 'Goldschleier' bears soft lacy tufts of golden seed heads.

DESCHAMPSIA CAESPITOSA

(dess-CHAMP-see-uh)

Tufted hair grass

- ■ Fine textured
- ■ Long-lasting flowers
- ■ Shade and drought tolerant
- ■ Zones 4–8

A graceful grass of glistening, silver-tinged purple spikelets that grows 2 to 3 feet tall. Excellent choice for the seaside garden. May self-seed.
USES: This grass provides year-round interest and is especially attractive with hostas or ferns. In mild-winter areas, leaves turn bronzy yellow and stay evergreen.
SITING AND CARE: Best in partial shade in damp soil but adjusts to varied situations. Work in compost or aged manure before planting in dry soil. Space 18 inches apart. Remove previous year's growth before new growth begins. Does not perform well in hot, humid conditions.

RECOMMENDED VARIETIES: 'Bronzeschleier' ('Bronze Veil') grows 2 to 3 feet tall with bronze-yellow tinted flowers and a high heat tolerance. 'Goldgehänge' ('Gold Shower') has handsome dark green leaves and spikelets that age to a rich golden yellow.

DIANTHUS

(dye-AN-thus)

Carnation, pink

10"
18"

- Cheerful colors, spring through early summer
- Attractive, grasslike foliage
- Spicy fragrance
- Zones 3–8

Flowers are pink, red, or white, often with a contrasting eye. This group includes plants from tiny creepers to 2-foot-tall cut flowers.
USES: An old-fashioned favorite, ideal for the cottage garden, the rock garden, or border front. Taller varieties are superb for cutting.

SITING AND CARE: Plant 6 to 15 inches apart, depending on mature height, in full sun in well-drained, neutral or alkaline soil. Shear flowers after blooming to encourage new growth and prevent reseeding.

RECOMMENDED VARIETIES AND RELATED SPECIES: Sweet William (*D. barbatus*) is a biennial or short-lived perennial that bears flat-topped flower clusters on 12- to 24-inch stems. *D. deltoides* 'Zing Rose' forms a 6-inch evergreen mat covered with rose-red flowers. *D. gratianopolitanus* 'Bath's Pink' performs well, even in hot, humid climates, with bountiful pink flowers on 10-inch-tall plants. *D.* ×

allwoodii 'Doris' is a free-flowering carnation with wonderfully fragrant salmon-pink flowers.

The gray-green foliage of garden pinks make an attractive foil for the fringed and lacy 1-inch flowers.

DIASCIA

(dye-ASH-ee-uh)

Twinspur

10"
12"

- Smothered in blooms, spring through early fall
- Summer-long color
- Low clumps
- Zones 8–9

Diminutive flowers (1 inch or less) bloom in showy clusters. Diascia is perennial in warm climates, but can be grown as an annual in zones 7 and colder.
USES: Touchy to grow but worth the effort. Where winter hardy, the plant cascades over rock walls.

Good container plant in the North.
SITING AND CARE: Plant in sun or partial shade in rich, moist, well-drained soil. Plant 15 inches apart. Water to keep moist, but guard against overwatering. Don't divide. Take cuttings to ensure survival. In the South, plant in the fall and enjoy flowers in the spring.

RECOMMENDED VARIETIES: *D. barberae* 'Ruby Field', the most popular hybrid, is 10 to 12 inches tall with handsome rose-colored flowers. *D. lilacina* 'Langthorn Lavender' has lilac-colored flowers produced heavily on 12-inch-tall stems. 'Blackthorn Apricot' has apricot-colored flowers on 12-inch plants. Rigid twinspur (*D. rigescens*)

is a robust species, 1 to 2 feet tall, with 6- to 8-inch-long trusses of spurred rosy pink flowers.

Snapdragon-like flowers of twinspur cover branching stems in clusters.

DICENTRA SPECTABILIS

(dye-SEN-tra)

Bleeding heart

30"
18"

- Heart-shaped spring blossoms
- Arching stems
- Classic, old-fashioned favorite
- Zones 2–8

Delicate, arching stems with dangling pink, red, white, purple, or yellow hearts brighten fine-textured, 30-inch-tall foliage.
USES: This much-loved perennial is spectacular in the woodland garden and good for cutting.

Bleeding heart looks best as a single specimen planted among ferns and other woodland plants, which fill in gaps when it goes dormant.
SITING AND CARE: Plant in filtered shade in rich, moist, well-drained soil. Cut back to the ground when dormancy begins. Division is not recommended.

RELATED SPECIES AND HYBRIDS: 'Alba', a white-flowered variety, is less vigorous than *D. spectabilis*, but quite lovely. Fringed bleeding heart (*D. eximia*), native to acid soils in the eastern U.S., has lovely pink flowers on foot-tall plants. 'Luxuriant' blooms from late spring to early fall without dormancy, with continuous cherry

red flowers on ferny, foot-tall plants. 'Margery Fish' blooms white, with 15-inch-tall, blue-green foliage.

Old-fashioned bleeding heart (above); 'Luxuriant' fringed bleeding heart (right).

DIGITALIS PURPUREA

(di-ji-TAL-is)

Foxglove

- Charming bell shaped flowers, late spring, early summer
- Cottage garden favorite
- Outstanding vertical effect
- Zones 4–8

The tall spikes of colorful bells of the foxglove open from bottom to top.

Actually a biennial, this 2- to 5-foot species self-sows so well you can count on its permanent presence.
USES: This is a charming, statuesque plant for woodland gardens, with colorful pink, purple, red, white, and yellow flowers. Good cut flower. Perfect for informal gardens, where foxglove can self-sow at abandon.
SITING AND CARE: Plant in partial to deep shade in moist, rich, acid, well-drained soil. Leaves are poisonous. Sow seeds outdoors without covering in late spring or early summer for blooms the following year, or set plants 18 to 24 inches apart in the fall.

RECOMMENDED VARIETIES AND RELATED SPECIES: Excelsior hybrids come in a mix of pastel pink, rose, white, and yellow, with tightly packed flowers and are 5 feet tall. 'Alba' is a white form that naturalizes well. *D. grandiflora* is the true perennial type, 2 to 3 feet tall with tubular yellow flowers. Strawberry foxglove (*D. × mertonensis*) has 5- to 7-foot-tall spires of coppery rose flowers.

DORONICUM ORIENTALE (OR CAUCASICUM)

(doh-RON-i-cum)

Leopard's bane

- Cheerful yellow spring flowers
- Heart-shaped foliage
- Good cut flower
- Zones 4–7

Leopard's bane's yellow blossoms signal spring in the shade garden.

Clusters of yellow flowers stand 15 to 24 inches tall in late spring, covering mounded, heart-shaped, dark green leaves. Doesn't tolerate heat in the South and falls dormant in summer after bloom.
USES: A daisy for shade is an uncommon find. Easy to grow. Interplant with ferns to mask bare spots left in summer.
SITING AND CARE: Plant in light to medium shade in rich, moist soil high in organic matter. Space plants 12 to 15 inches apart. Mulch to conserve soil moisture; water during dry spring weather.
RECOMMENDED VARIETIES: 'Finesse' has semidouble, yellow-orange flowers on 15-inch stems. 'Magnificum' forms neat, 15-inch mounds with bright yellow flowers on 2½-foot-tall stems. 'Miss' ('Madame Mason') is 1 to 2 feet tall with canary yellow daisy flowers and more persistent foliage than the species.

DRYOPTERIS FILIX-MAS

(dry-OP-ter-is)

Male wood fern

- Easy fern to grow
- Tolerates dry soil
- Forms substantial clumps
- Zones 4–8

The large, firm, dark green fronds of male wood fern are finely cut.

Sturdy and masculine compared to the delicate lady fern, this plant grows to four feet tall.
USES: Handsome and adaptable, male wood fern is a favorite for the shady woodland setting where it has room to show off. Attractive in the garden border in combination with toad lily (*Tricyrtis*) or bleeding heart (*Dicentra*).
SITING AND CARE: Plant in shade or filtered sun in neutral to acid, fertile soil. Space 2 feet apart. Can be quite sun tolerant. Replenish organic matter. Divide larger clumps regularly. If new plants are not divided, the symmetry of the fern may be lost, and it will become a large clump, which many consider attractive. Fronds persist into winter.
RECOMMENDED VARIETIES AND RELATED SPECIES: 'Crispa' is a dwarf form with crested fronds. 'Cristata' has divided and crested frond tips. 'Linearis' bears fronds with slender, linear divisions. Autumn fern (*D. erythrosora*) is a colorful evergreen with coppery-red new growth that holds its color until mature then changes to a deep glossy green. Hardy in zones 5 to 9.

ECHINACEA PURPUREA

(ek-i-NAY-see-uh)

Purple coneflower

3'
2'

- Bold, colorful daisies, midsummer to fall
- Heat tolerant
- Prairie native
- Zones 3–8

Magnificent daisylike flowers that bloom on 2- to 4-foot plants make this one of the finest perennials for today's gardens.

USES: Unsurpassed for summer show, this easy-to-grow plant tolerates heat and drought.

SITING AND CARE: Best in full sun but adapts to partial shade. Plant in lean, well-drained soil. Purple coneflower is easily naturalized in wildflower gardens. Or back it with Russian sage (*Perovskia*) or ornamental grasses. Excellent cut flower. Space plants 18 to 24 inches apart. Rejuvenate clumps by division in early spring every third or fourth year. Deadhead to promote rebloom or leave cones for late-season interest.

RECOMMENDED VARIETIES: 'Bravado' features huge, 6-inch, rose-purple blossoms. 'Magnus' has flat, carmine-colored petals. 'White Swan' is 2 to 3 feet tall with white flowers; also excellent for cutting. 'White Lustre' differs from 'White Swan' in having a more orange-bronze center as well as more horizontal petals.

A popular favorite, purple coneflower is one of the finest garden plants.

ECHINOPS BANNATICUS

(EK-i-nops)

Globe thistle

3'
2'

- Showy blue spheres in midsummer
- Large, dramatic plants
- Distinctive dried
- Zones 3–7

Globe thistle provides a long-lasting show. Individual flowers are bunched together in steely blue, globelike heads. A tall plant reaching 3 to 4 feet tall, it is heat tolerant and thrives in southern gardens.

USES: Easy-to-grow drama for poor, dry soils. Pair it with white phlox or threadleaf coreopsis.

SITING AND CARE: Prefers full sun but tolerates light shade. Plant in well-drained, average soil. Space 18 to 24 inches apart. Division is difficult but sometimes necessary in spring if clumps are crowded. Aphids are a serious pest. Flowers are prickly to the touch.

RECOMMENDED VARIETIES AND RELATED SPECIES: 'Blue Globe' bears steel blue flowers. *E. ritro* 'Taplow Blue' has silver-blue globes; 'Veitch's Blue' produces dark blue, slightly smaller spheres. *E. sphaerocephalus* 'Arctic Glow' has white globes on 30-inch stems.

The blue flowers and bold, spiny leaves of 'Taplow Blue' globe thistle.

EPIMEDIUM X RUBRUM

(eh-pi-MEE-dee-um)

Red barrenwort

10"
12"

- Dainty spring flowers
- Great ground cover
- Autumn color
- Zones 5–8

This slow spreader has a long season of interest, from its small red spring blossoms to foot-tall autumn mounds of attractive bronze leaves. Heart-shaped leaves remain evergreen in milder parts of its range.

USES: Barrenwort is one of the few plants that tolerates dry shade under trees and shrubs. Use as an excellent ground cover around azaleas and other shade-loving flowering shrubs.

SITING AND CARE: Plant in partial to full shade in fertile, well-drained soil. Space plants 12 inches apart. Keep soil moist until established. Remember to shear back old leaves in early spring.

RELATED SPECIES: *E. × versicolor* 'Sulphureum' is a vigorous spreader with pale yellow flowers. *E. grandiflorum* has pale pink flowers of a larger size than *E. × rubrum*. *E. × perralchicum* 'Fröhnleiten' is a robust form, 4 to 8 inches tall, with excellent yellow flowers held well above the foliage. *E. × youngianum* 'Niveum' bears white flowers on 6- to 8-inch plants.

Also known as bishop's hat, barrenwort thrives in the woodland.

ERIGERON HYBRIDS

(eh-RIH-juh-rawn)

Fleabane

Erigeron 'Adria' is a choice front tier plant for bright blue flowers.

2'

2'

- Wide range of colors, midsummer to fall
- Tough and adaptable
- Excellent for cutting
- Zones 4–9 (zone 7 east of the Rocky Mountains)

This dainty yet bushy North American native looks like aster, but is even easier to grow. And it blooms earlier.

USES: Fleabane is a care-free plant for the front or middle of a sunny border. Plant in drifts of three or more with irises for season-long color and contrasting shapes.

SITING AND CARE: Best in full sun and in sandy, well-drained soil. Plant 12 to 18 inches apart. Cut back after flowering to reduce weediness and rejuvenate the foliage. Taller varieties may require staking. Divide every three years.

RECOMMENDED VARIETIES: *E. speciosus* 'Azure Fairy' (also called 'Azure Beauty') is 30 inches tall with semidouble lavender-blue flowers. 'Rosa Triumph' is 24 inches tall, clear pink, with large double flowers; 'Dimity' is a dwarf pink, 12 inches tall; 'Foerster's Darling' ('Foerster's Liebling') is 16 inches tall and has semidouble, deep pink flowers. *E. karvinskianus* is a dwarf, trailing plant, which bears lovely masses of white to pink flowers all summer. It is best in zones 8 to 9, but reseeds freely further north.

Amythyst-blue, thistlelike sea holly blooms on deeply colored stems.

ERYNGIUM AMETHYSTINUM

(eh-RIN-jee-um)

Sea holly

2'

2'

- Striking effect
- Profuse, showy, mid-summer flowers
- Long-lasting in flower arrangements
- Zones 2–8

Stiff and prickly, this easy-care, 2-foot-tall plant with steely blue flowers seldom needs staking. It is ideal for dry, sandy soils.

USES: Its handsome form provides interesting contrast in the midborder combined with wormwood (*Artemisia*) or yellow varieties of yarrow (*Achillea*). Tolerance to salt spray makes sea holly a good candidate for a seaside garden. Extremely cold tolerant.

SITING AND CARE: Plant in full sun in well-drained soil. Sow seeds in spring or set nursery plants 15 to 18 inches apart. Taproot makes plants difficult to move or divide.

RELATED SPECIES: *E. alpinum* 'Blue Star' grows 2 to 3 feet tall with large lavender-blue flowers that resemble fireworks. *E. planum* 'Blaukappe' blooms all summer with intense blue flowers. *E. × oliverianum* is 3 feet tall with pale blue flowers and deeply cut foliage.

The massive, rose-purple clusters of Joe-Pye weed 'Gateway' bloom profusely on six-foot mottled stems.

EUPATORIUM PURPUREUM

(yew-pa-TOR-ee-um)

Joe-Pye weed

6'

3'

- Late summer dusky rose blossoms
- Sturdy garden giant
- Butterfly magnet
- Zones 3–8

This bold native eastern roadside plant grows 6 to 8 feet tall.

USES: Joe-Pye weed is a must for the butterfly garden and ideal for back of the border or naturalized in a meadow garden. Plant it with butterfly weed (*Asclepias*) for a dynamite butterfly duo. This plant is not for the small urban garden.

SITING AND CARE: Plant in full sun to light shade in moist soil. Set plants 3 feet apart or sow seeds. To control height, pinch back in early summer, if desired. Thin to improve air circulation if mildew is a problem. Divide overcrowded clumps in spring.

RECOMMENDED VARIETIES AND RELATED SPECIES: 'Atropurpureum' has purple stems, flowers, and leaves. 'Gateway' has mauve-pink flowers and grows 5 to 6 feet tall. *E. fistulosum* 'Bartered Bride' is a white form. Hardy ageratum (*Conoclinium coelestinum*) is 2 to 3 feet tall with bluish purple flowers. Zones 6 to 10.

EUPHORBIA POLYCHROMA

(yew-FOR-bee-uh)

Cushion spurge

15"
18"

- Showy yellow spring flowers
- Neat, mounding habit, pest free
- Attractive summer foliage
- Zones 4–8 (zone 7 east of the Rocky Mountains)

This easy-to-grow, front-of-the-border plant can become invasive in fertile, moist conditions.
USES: Cushion spurge is a knockout and looks like yellow cushions in spring.
SITING AND CARE: Plant 15 to 18 inches apart in full sun (or afternoon shade in the South) in well-drained, sandy soil of average fertility. Handle carefully; stem sap is irritating to skin.
RELATED SPECIES: Myrtle spurge (*E. myrsinites*) is an evergreen trailing plant with sulphur yellow bracts on 8- to 10-inch stems. Mediterranean spurge (*E. characias ssp. wulfenii*) has upright stems 3 to 4 feet tall. Zones 7 to 9. Griffith's spurge (*E. griffithii*) has many brick red bracts above green leaves with pale pink midribs. Zones 5 to 7.

Myrtle spurge tolerates heat well.

The light green foliage of cushion spurge is topped with yellow bracts.

Mediterranean (above) and Griffith's spurge (right).

FESTUCA GLAUCA

(fess-TOO-ka)

Dwarf blue fescue

8"
8"

- Silvery-blue foliage
- Good for contrast
- Evergreen
- Zones 4–8

The slender blades of this attractive grass grow 6 to 10 inches tall.
USES: This lovely small plant offers good contrast in rock gardens or when paired with hardy geraniums or threadleaf coreopsis (*Coreopsis verticillata* 'Moonbeam').
SITING AND CARE: Plant in full sun or light shade in well-drained soil. Space 8 inches apart. Divide every other year and remove flowers to prolong plant's life.
RECOMMENDED VARIETIES: 'Elijah Blue' is an excellent form with 8- to 12-inch powdery blue leaves. Hard-to-find 'Solling' is a nonflowering form, 6 to 10 inches tall with beautiful blue-gray foliage.

Handsome tufts of dwarf blue fescue.

FILIPENDULA RUBRA

(fi-li-PEN-dew-la)

Queen-of-the-prairie

7'
4'

- Sturdy and stately
- Wetlands native
- Beautiful seed heads
- Zones 3–9 (zone 7 east of the Rocky Mountains)

Queen-of-the-prairie looks something like a giant astilbe when it blooms. Large 4- to 7-foot plants support huge, jagged leaves.
USES: It is perfect for that wet area where water stands after every rain, and its height makes it queen of the border. Show it off in wildflower gardens or at the back of the border. Excellent with bee balm (*Monarda*), Joe-Pye weed (*Eupatorium*), or false indigo (*Baptisia*).
SITING AND CARE: Plant in sun or partial shade in rich, moist soil. Space plants 24 to 30 inches apart. Water if necessary to keep soil moist. Plants stressed by dry soil are prone to mildew. Staking is not necessary. Dig and divide clumps only if they're crowded.
RECOMMENDED VARIETIES AND RELATED SPECIES: 'Venusta' grows 4 to 6 feet tall with fragrant rose flowers. *F. vulgaris* 'Flore Pleno' has creamy white plumes on 12- to 24-inch plants. Siberian meadowsweet (*F. palmata*) is 3 to 4 feet tall with 6-inch-wide flattened heads of pale pink flowers.

Feathery pink, cotton-candy plumes of Filipendula rubra 'Venusta'.

'Goblin' blanket flower is valued for its midsummer range of hot colors.

GAILLARDIA X GRANDIFLORA

(gay-LAR-dee-uh)

Blanket flower

- ■ Bold, bright summer-long daisies
- ■ Gray-green foliage
- ■ Tolerates heat and drought conditions
- ■ Zones 2–9

Ideal for the West or seaside garden, this wildflower grows from 1 to 3 feet, depending on the variety.
USES: Blanket flower will give you easy, long-lasting color in a sunny border and poor soil. Good for cutting. Use with goldenrod (Solidago) or ornamental grasses.
SITING AND CARE: Plant in full sun in soil of poor to average fertility with good drainage. Space 12 to 15 inches apart. Taller varieties may require staking, and occasional removal of spent flowers may be necessary. Divide every two or three years in spring.
RECOMMENDED VARIETIES: 'Baby Cole' is a dwarf type with red-banded flowers. 'Burgundy' is 30 inches tall with wine-red flowers. 'Dazzler' grows 30 inches tall with crimson tips on yellow-centered flowers. 'Goblin' is a wonderfully petite 12 inches and has dark red petals tipped with yellow.

GERANIUM SANGUINEUM

(je-RAY-nee-um)

Bloody cranesbill

- ■ Magenta flowers, early summer to fall
- ■ Red autumn foliage
- ■ Pretty as ground cover
- ■ Zones 3–8

The bright blue flowers of Geranium × 'Johnson's Blue' are excellent as a ground cover.

This is not the annual geranium (Pelargonium) popular for pots but a long-lived perennial that blooms sporadically until fall in some areas.
USES: Great for care-free color in the front border or as a blooming ground cover. A favorite with garden designers. Best for smaller gardens. Very hardy in southern gardens. Pretty with columbine (Aquilegia) or iris. Charming as a ground cover under shrubs.
SITING AND CARE: Plant in sun or partial shade in any well-drained soil. (Full sun is necessary for best autumn color; partial shade required in the South.) Space 15 inches apart. Seldom needs division, and pests and diseases aren't usually a problem. Cut back after first bloom to promote rebloom.
RECOMMENDED VARIETIES AND RELATED SPECIES: G. cinereum 'Ballerina' has 2-inch pink blossoms with purple veining and dark centers on 6-inch plants. Zones 5 to 7. G. macrorrhizum 'Ingwersen's Variety' is soft pink, 12 inches tall. Zone 4. G. psilostemon 'Bressingham Flair' has lilac-pink flowers on 3-foot-tall plants. Zones 4 to 6. G. sanguineum striatum is light pink, 6 to 8 inches tall. 'Album' is pure white, 10 to 12 inches tall. 'Johnson's Blue' is a long-blooming, 18-inch-tall hybrid with prolific blue-violet flowers. Zones 4 to 7. The Geranium genus is large, and offers innumerable species and varieties to delight the gardener. Only a few of the many choices are mentioned here.

Geranium sanguineum 'Lancastriense' tolerates heat and cold better than the other species.

Geranium sanguineum 'Alpenglow' grows about 8 inches tall with vivid rose-red blossoms. Zones 3 to 8.

The foliage of many varieties of hardy geranium provide autumn color, turning yellow and vivid red.

GEUM HYBRIDS

JEE-um)

Geum

- Electric colors, late spring through summer
- Attractive foliage
- Great for cutting
- Zones 3–7

Bright red, orange, and yellow flowers bloom on dark green foliage. **USES:** Geum's showy display of eye-catching colors is good at the front of the border, backed by the cool blues of delphinium or bellflower (*Campanula*). **SITING AND CARE:** Best performance is in full sun in cool regions. Where summers are hot, afternoon shade is mandatory. Requires humus-rich soil with excellent drainage for long-term survival. Plant 12 to 18 inches apart. Water abundantly during the growing season. Deadhead to prolong bloom season. No serious pests or diseases if plants are sited right. Division is seldom required. **RECOMMENDED VARIETIES:** Heavy-flowering 'Borisii' is pure scarlet-orange, 10 inches tall. G. *chiloense* 'Lady Stratheden' has buttercup yellow blooms on 15-inch plants; 'Mrs. Bradshaw' produces scarlet, semidouble flowers on plants 1 to 2 feet tall.

Scarlet blossoms of 'Mrs. Bradshaw' geum nod above frilly leaves.

GUNNERA MANICATA

(GUN-er-rah)

Gunnera

- Umbrella-size leaves
- Dramatic
- Tropical
- Zone 7–10, zone 6 with winter protection

Coarse mounds of enormous 4-foot-wide leaves grow to a colossal 6 to 8 feet tall. A plant only for mild-winter, cool-summer climates. **USES:** Gunnera is perfect for poolside or accent. Combine it with finer-textured perennials such as astilbe or Siberian iris. **SITING AND CARE:** Grow in sun or partial shade in moist or wet, fertile soil. Allow 8 feet between plants. Keep soil moist and fertilize at regular intervals. Gunnera does not perform well in climates where temperatures reach over 80°F. Grows in bogs, shallow water, and stream banks. If not provided with adequate moisture, gunnera leaves turn brown and dry up. **RELATED SPECIES:** G. *magellanica* has smaller, 2-foot-wide, dark green, kidney-shaped leaves and is a favorite swampy ground cover. G. *tinctoria* is slightly smaller, at 6 feet tall, and has reddish flowers hidden among the foliage.

Gunnera: drama for large spaces.

GYPSOPHILA PANICULATA

(jip-SOFF-i-luh)

Baby's breath

- Billows of white
- Airy and delicate
- Excellent cut or dried
- Zones 3–7

Baby's breath, a ubiquitous component of floral arrangements, is a charming, easy-to-grow addition in the home landscape. **USES:** Baby's breath makes a gorgeous background for other summer-blooming perennials and is perfect with foxglove (*Digitalis*) or lilies. A definite must for the cut-flower garden. **SITING AND CARE:** Plant in full sun in lean, sandy, well-drained, alkaline soil (add lime if soil is acidic). Space 3 feet apart. Provide wire support. Division is not recommended. **RECOMMENDED VARIETIES AND RELATED SPECIES:** 'Bristol Fairy' has double white flowers and grows 2 to 3 feet tall. 'Flamingo' grows 3 to 4 feet tall and bears double pink flowers. 'Perfecta' has large double white flowers. Creeping baby's breath (*Gypsophila repens*) is a wonderful plant for the front border that grows only 6 to 12 inches tall with white to lilac flowers. Good for edging. G. *repens* 'Rosea' is 8 inches tall with pale pink flowers.

The cloudlike mist of 'Bristol Fairy' baby's breath covers graceful foliage.

Yellow variegated golden grass is one of the best grasses for shade.

HAKONECHLOA MACRA 'AUREOLA'

(ha-kon-eh-KLOH-ah)

Golden grass

Golden grass is prized for its handsome fall and winter color.

12"

18"

- Handsome pinkish red fall color and bronze winter color
- Good grass for shade
- Slow creeper
- Zones 6 –7

This foot-tall plant is slow to establish but worth the wait, eventually forming a dense mass. **USES:** Its bright yellow markings light up shady gardens and are smashing with hosta, especially 'Aureomarginata' with its yellow-bordered, dark green leaves. **SITING AND CARE:** Plant in filtered light in a humus-rich, well-drained, acid soil. Space 12 to 15 inches apart.

'Moerheim Beauty' is a bright rusty-red cultivar of Helen's flower.

HELENIUM AUTUMNALE

(he-LEE-nee-um)

Helen's flower

4'

3'

- Bold, hot colors
- Late summer blooms
- Sturdy plants
- Adaptable
- Zones 3–7

Native to wet meadows of eastern North America, Helen's flower grows 3 to 5 feet tall, depending on moisture and variety, and blooms for 8 to 10 weeks. **USES:** Helen's flower lends the border a late-summer color boost and combines well with asters or ornamental grasses.

SITING AND CARE: Plant in full sun in lean, moist soil high in organic matter. Space 18 to 24 inches apart. Stake taller varieties. Cut back after flowering to keep disease and insects at bay. Divide plants when crowded, usually every other year. Fertilize sparingly. **RECOMMENDED VARIETIES:** 'Moerheim Beauty' blooms rusty red, changing to orange and then gold on 2- to 3-foot plants. 'Rotgold' (Red and Gold Hybrid) has red and gold flowers on 3- to 4-foot plants. 'Brilliant' produces large numbers of bronze flowers. 'Wyndley' is only 2 to 3 feet tall with coppery brown flowers.

HELIANTHUS X MULTIFLORUS

(hee-lee-AN-thus)

Easy-to-grow perennial sunflower 'Triomphe de Gard' produces flowers that last four to six weeks into fall.

Perennial sunflower

5'

4'

- Late-summer gold blossoms
- Sturdy plant
- Flowers are good for cutting
- Long-lived
- Zones 4–8

Valued for late-season effect on statuesque, 5- to 7-foot plants. **USES:** Perennial sunflower is a dependable back-of-the-border plant that makes a good backdrop for purple coneflower (*Echinacea*) or butterfly weed (*Asclepias*).

SITING AND CARE: Best in full sun but tolerates partial shade. Plant in humus-rich, well-drained, neutral to alkaline soil. Space 2 to 3 feet apart. Stake taller varieties. Be sure to divide when crowded, usually every three or four years. **RECOMMENDED VARIETIES AND RELATED SPECIES:** 'Flore Pleno' has double yellow flowers that look like dahlias. 'Loddon Gold' produces yellow pompon-style flowers. *H. angustifolius*, swamp sunflower, grows 5 to 7 feet with brown-centered yellow flowers in late fall. Zones 6 to 9. Willow-leaved sunflower (*H. salicifolius*) is similar with narrower leaves, and is hardy to zone 4.

HELICTOTRICHON SEMPERVIRENS

(heh-lik-toh-TRY-kon)

Blue oat grass

30"

- Spiky habit
- Arching, oatlike
- 30" flowers
- Easy care
- Zones 4–9

This tall grass looks something like blue fescue but forms much bigger, 24-inch clumps. Flowers start off brownish, then turn to a golden wheat color in fall.

USES: Attractive foliage and beautiful form. Good as a specimen or in mass plantings. Works well in situations where blue-gray foliage is necessary to "cool" the garden. Makes an excellent companion for obedient plant (*Physostegia*) or coral bells (*Heuchera*).

SITING AND CARE: Plant in full sun in well-drained, neutral to slightly alkaline soil. Attractive in masses. Space 2 or 3 feet apart. Cut back by half in late winter and divide every third year. It is prone to fungal attack in humid climates. Winter mulch is recommended north of zone 5.

RECOMMENDED VARIETIES: 'Saphirsprudel' (Sapphire Fountain) has bluer leaves than the species and is more weather tolerant.

Blue oat grass is grown for striking blue foliage like a large blue fescue.

HELIOPSIS HELIANTHOIDES SCABRA

(hee-lee-OP-sis)

False sunflower

4'

- Blooms July to frost
- Lush green leaves
- Easy and long-lived
- Zones 3–9

2'

This bushy plant with 3-inch pale yellow flowers is a prairie native. It grows 3 or 4 feet tall.

USES: Bright, solid color and long bloom time make this plant indispensable in informal borders. Good for cutting. Combine false sunflower with false indigo (*Baptisia*) or speedwell (*Veronica*).

SITING AND CARE: Plant in full sun in well-drained soil. Space plants 2 feet apart. Fertilize sparingly. Staking is necessary, especially if plants are shaded. Divide every two or three years.

RECOMMENDED VARIETIES: 'Karat' has extra-large, clear yellow, single blossoms. 'Gold Greenheart' is 3 feet tall with very showy, interesting green-centered, double, chrome yellow flowers. 'Summer Sun' has delightful bright gold, semidouble flowers, and its superior heat tolerance makes it the best cultivar for southern gardens. It also doesn't get too leggy.

False sunflower is native to the dry prairies of North America.

HELLEBORUS ORIENTALIS

(heh-leh-BORE-us)

Lenten rose

15"

- Dusky rose or white blooms late winter, early spring
- Glossy green leaves
- Flowers are good for cutting
- Zones 4–9

15"

Clumps of handsome foliage are evergreen in all but the coldest parts of their range.

USES: An early delight for winter-weary gardeners, lenten rose is one of the finest low-growing plants in cultivation. It's a wonderful addition to the woodland garden under the canopy of deciduous trees, with small, early bulbs (such as grape hyacinth or snowdrop) and astilbe.

SITING AND CARE: Plant in full to partial shade in a protected spot. Best in rich, moist, well-drained soil enriched with organic material. Space 2 feet apart. Division is not recommended.

RELATED SPECIES: Bear's foot hellebore (*H. foetidus*), named for its fingerlike evergreen leaves, has pale green, purple-rimmed flowers in late winter or very early spring; zones 5 to 8. Christmas rose (*H. niger*) has late-winter pink flowers, tinged white; zones 3 to 7.

The late-winter flowers of Lenten rose open over leathery leaves.

HEMEROCALLIS HYBRIDS

(heh-mer-oh-KAL-is)

Daylily

- Easy, dependable mid-summer color
- Quite adaptable and long-lived
- Handsome, straplike foliage
- Zones 3–9

Available in virtually every color of the rainbow except blue, daylily flowers may be plain or ruffled, striped or bicolored, single or double. Heights range from 10-inch minis to 40-inch giants. Some varieties, best for southern regions, are evergreen. Peak time for flowers is in midsummer, but some varieties rebloom. A few superstars bloom from late spring to fall frost.

USES: Showy but easy, daylilies are a gardener's dream. Versatile plants blend beautifully with most other perennials. One perfect partner is the cheerful shasta daisy (*Leucanthemum × superbum*).

SITING AND CARE: Plant in full sun or partial shade. Afternoon shade is recommended in the South. Daylilies aren't picky but grow best in humus-rich and well-drained soil. Plant anytime during the growing season (even when plants are in bloom!). Allow 18 inches to 3 feet between plants, depending on the variety. Divide every three to five years, when the number of blossoms begins to decline.

RECOMMENDED VARIETIES: 'Happy Returns' has lemon yellow flowers and reblooms in all climates, hot or cold. 'Pardon Me' is a vigorous bright red rebloomer with a yellow throat. 'Stella de Oro' has become particularly popular, with blooms of golden yellow that put on a show over an incredibly long season, spring to frost.

'Becky Lynn' offers fragrant rose-pink blooms.

'Frans Hals' has rusty red petals with orange sepals.

Beloved 'Stella De Oro' reblooms yellow-orange.

'Dominic' bears blooms in very dark black-red.

Slow-growing 'Ruffled Apricot' has apricot petals.

Free-flowering 'Prairie Blue Eyes' is lavender-blue.

'Scarlet Orbit' is bright red with a yellow-green throat.

Star-shaped 'Hyperion' bears slender yellow petals.

Pale orange-pink 'Fairy Tale Pink' is ruffled.

'Smoky Mountain Autumn' has a lavender-pink halo.

Each showy, trumpet-shaped daylily blossom lasts merely a day, but new buds continue to open for weeks.

HEUCHERA HYBRIDS

(HYOO-keh-ra)

Coral bells

20"
20"

■ Dainty, bell-shaped flowers in late spring, early summer
■ Decorative foliage
■ Zones 3–8 (varies with specific varieties)

An old-fashioned favorite loved for its wiry-stemmed, white or pink summer flowers, coral bells hybrids now have striking-colored foliage that is ruffled, lobed, or marbled with contrasting veins.
USES: This small package (1 to 2 feet tall) is appealing as bedding, edging, and in front of the border.
SITING AND CARE: Plant in full sun or partial shade, in moist, well-drained, humus-rich soil. Space plants 12 to 18 inches apart. Deadhead to promote rebloom. In winter, cover with loose covering, such as evergreen boughs, to prevent frost heaving. Divide every three or four years.
RECOMMENDED VARIETIES: 'Palace Purple' has rich mahogany red leaves and small white flowers. 'Pewter Moon' has pink flowers, maroon stems, and leaves marbled with pewter on top, deep maroon on underside. 'Raspberry Regal' produces extra-large, raspberry red flowers, ideal for cutting, and green marbled foliage. Exciting new varieties are continually being introduced into the market.

Beautiful mounds of attractive foliage produce airy clusters of coral bells, making this a garden favorite.

HIBISCUS MOSCHEUTOS

(hih-BISS-kus)

Rose mallow

5'
3'

■ Huge, dramatic flowers bloom midsummer to frost
■ Tall, husky plants
■ Maplelike foliage
■ Zones 5–9

With its large maple-like leaves and gigantic, dinner-plate-size, pink, red, or white flowers, this 4- to 8-foot plant looks like it's from the tropics.
USES: This marshland native is an impressive but easy-to-grow plant, ideal for a moist location.
SITING AND CARE: Grows best in wet, humus-rich soil but also adapts to ordinary garden soil. Plant in full sun or partial shade. Space plants 2 to 3 feet apart. No staking needed. Water in dry weather. Handpick Japanese beetles (they are a severe pest). Mark location; plants are late to emerge in spring. Not necessary to divide. Easy from seed.
RECOMMENDED VARIETIES: The Disco Belle Series comes in pink, rosy red, or white, with 9-inch flowers on compact plants 20 to 30 inches tall. 'Lady Baltimore' has pink, 8-inch flowers with satiny red centers, on 4- to 6-foot plants. 'Lord Baltimore' blooms brilliant red with 10-inch flowers. 'Southern Belle' comes in a mix of colors from white to dark rose-red with 10- or 12-inch flowers on compact, 3- to 4-foot-tall plants.

The huge blossoms of 'Disco Belle' can reach the size of dinner plates.

IMPERATA CYLINDRICA 'RED BARON'

(im-per-AH-ta)

Japanese blood grass

15"
24"

■ Brilliant red foliage
■ Intensified fall color
■ Non-flowering
■ Spreads rapidly
■ Zones 6–9

'Red Baron' grows in upright clumps 12 to 18 inches tall and, in cooler climates, gets redder as the season progresses. Not for hot, dry areas. Can be invasive. Mass it with silver-gray plants, such as lamb's-ears *(Stachys)*, or grow in containers with other perennials.
USES: Its beautiful red color backed by sunlight is unforgettable. Japanese blood grass is better adapted to tubs and containers with other companion plants. Provides excellent fall red color.
SITING AND CARE: Plant in full sun for best color, in moist, well-drained soil. Plant 12 to 15 inches apart. Dig out any green grass that appears. Occasionally it transforms to its green-leaved parent, and those shoots should be eliminated aggressively. The farther south this grass is planted, the less the red color is evident.

Blood grass is bright red all summer.

(HOSS-ta)

Hosta

- Lush, bold foliage
- Lily-like summer blossoms
- Queen of the shade
- Zones 3–8

Some are tiny plants a few inches wide, others are giants that sprawl 6 feet across or more. Hostas have showy leaves that are variegated, puckered or ruffled and vary from oval to oblong, narrow to wide. They are relatively care-free plants.

USES: This is an intriguing group of plants for the woodland garden. Use as ground cover or edging. Pair with astilbe, corydalis, or ferns for an enticing contrast of textures.

SITING AND CARE: Plant in dappled shade in moist, well-drained, humus-rich soil. Enrich soil with compost or aged manure before planting. Water in dry weather until established. In cold regions, protect hostas the first winter with 1 to 2 inches of shredded leaves or other mulch. Divide crowded clumps in spring when tips emerge. Trap snails and slugs, or surround plants with a barrier of sand or copper strips.

RECOMMENDED VARIETIES AND RELATED SPECIES: August lily (H. plantaginea) has light green leaves and large, white, fragrant flowers. 'Frances Williams' (H. sieboldiana) is blue-green with golden borders, with white flowers. 'Sum and Substance' makes a large specimen plant with huge golden leaves and lavender flowers.

'Brigham Blue' pairs quite nicely with Carex elata 'Aurea'.

'Blue Mammoth' and 'Sun Power' display contrasting foliage.

Dueling variegation: 'Thomas Hogg' with Hosta undulata variegata.

'Gold Standard' makes a colorful, dramatic statement in two tones.

'Kabitan' is a miniature with lance-shaped yellow leaves, dark margins.

Hosta sieboldiana elegans sports huge, puckered, heart-shaped leaves.

Miniature hostas, such as 'Chartreuse Wiggles' (left) invite close inspection in the shade garden. The 1-inch flower of Primula sieboldii on the moss at lower right gives a hint of this hosta's tiny size.

IRIS HYBRIDS

(EYE-ris)

Bearded iris

- Rainbow of spring colors
- Large blossoms
- Swordlike leaves
- Zones 3–10

Named for Iris, the Greek goddess of the rainbow, irises come in almost every color imaginable, often with contrasting beards. Sizes range from 6-inch dwarfs to plants of 4 feet or more.

USES: Bearded iris flowers are favored for their showy structure, unlimited color combinations, and lovely fragrance. Combines well with bellflower (*Campanula*) or wormwood (*Artemisia*).

SITING AND CARE: Plant in full sun to light shade in fertile, well-drained soil. Plant in July or August, when available. Space rhizomes 12 to 15 inches apart, with their newest leaves facing the direction you want the plant to grow. Cover with 1 inch of soil. Fertilize in early spring. Keep moist during active growth. Control leaf spot and borers by removing all dead leaves before new growth begins in spring. Divide every three or four years, or when flowering declines. Taller varieties may require staking. Mulches may be used if kept away from leaves and rhizomes.

RECOMMENDED VARIETIES AND RELATED SPECIES: Thousands of varieties are available, including these recent award winners: 'Beverly Sills' is a highly sought-after coral-pink variety that blooms on 35-inch stems. 'Conjuration' is 38-inches tall, bearing white flowers banded with violet. 'Dusky Challenger' has large ruffled flowers of very dark purple on vigorous 36-inch plants. 'Edith Wolford' is a bicolor with yellow standards and orange-tipped blue beards, 35 inches tall. 'Honky Tonk Blues' has ruffled violet-blue flowers swirled and edged with white and stands 36 inches tall. 'Silverado' is a cool blue-and-white on tall, sturdy 38-inch stems. *Iris foetidissima* 'Variegata' has variegated leaves.

Mixed in riotous masses, tall bearded iris create a kaleidoscope of color.

Showy bearded iris can brighten the border from spring to midsummer.

Burgundy-red 'Wine Master' must not be shaded by other plants.

'Dot 'n Dash' produces deep blue-violet flowers with a white splash.

'American Style' reveals pastel apricot standards, falls, and beards.

The stunning blossoms of 'Beguine' are vanilla blushed with maroon.

'Spinning Wheel' has clean white flowers speckled and edged in violet.

IRIS CRISTATA

(EYE-ris kris-ta-tuh)

Dwarf crested iris

Iris cristata *is one of the finest ground covers for difficult dry shade.*

- Pale lilac blue spring flowers with yellow crests
- Low, handsome foliage
- Shade tolerant
- Zones 3–8

This lovely, lightly fragrant iris naturalizes well and is a native of the southeastern U. S. Bright green 4- to 6-inch leaves emerge from a rhizome and spread in fan-shaped sprays. One to two pale blue blossoms are produced on each 2- to 3-inch-tall stem.

USES: This is one of the best plants for dry shade. It works well as a specimen or ground cover, spreading to make a low carpet of bloom. Pair it with bleeding heart (*Dicentra*) or columbine (*Aquilegia*).

SITING AND CARE: Plant 15 inches apart in partial sun to deep shade, although it will flourish with morning sun. Moist, well drained soils are best, but it will also thrive in dry conditions. Plant rhizomes or container-grown plants in spring. It looks spectacular massed in drifts in the woodland garden. Divide in fall, if desired.

RECOMMENDED VARIETIES: 'Alba' is a handsome white-flowered variety with contrasting yellow crests that is decidedly less vigorous than the species (and also not as common). 'Caerulea' is darker blue than the native form.

IRIS ENSATA

(EYE-ris en-sa-tuh)

Japanese iris

Showy, flat flowers of Japanese iris often grow to 10 inches across.

- Orchid-like flowers late spring or summer
- Tall, swordlike leaves
- Superb in moist soil
- Zones 4–9

Cool blues, purples, pinks, and white flowers bloom on sturdy stems 3 or 4 feet tall (up to 6 feet in rich, boggy soils in mild climates, but not in the dry heat of the Southwest).

USES: Excellent eyecatchers for boggy soils. Combine with queen-of-the-prairie (*Filipendula*).

SITING AND CARE: Plant in full sun or partial shade (partial shade required in the South). Provide a rich, acid soil and plenty of water when in bloom; conditions can be drier the rest of the year. Space 18 to 24 inches apart. Apply acid fertilizer occasionally. Division is rarely required.

RECOMMENDED VARIETIES AND RELATED SPECIES: 'Cry of Rejoice' has deep purple flowers with yellow centers. 'Great White Heron' bears large pure white flowers up to 11 inches across, on 4- to 5-inch-tall plants. 'Nikko' is only 18 to 20 inches tall with pale blue flowers veined in deep purple. 'Pink Frost' bears ruffled 8-inch-wide pink flowers. Yellow flag iris (*I. pseudacorus*) has beardless yellow flowers on stems 3 or 4 feet tall. It thrives in standing water or very moist soil. Zones 2 to 9.

IRIS SIBIRICA

(EYE-ris sye-BEER-i-kuh)

Siberian iris

Siberian iris 'White Swirl' bears bright, white flowers in summer.

- Broad range of colors in early summer
- Lush, grasslike leaves
- Easy and long-lived
- Zones 3–9

The flower show begins just after the bearded irises. Most varieties grow 2 or 3 feet tall.

USES: Unlike bearded iris, the foliage of this iris stays reliably green and lush all summer long. Lovely at the edge of a pond or in combination with lady's mantle (*Alchemilla*) or hardy geranium.

SITING AND CARE: Plant in full sun or partial shade. It tolerates almost any soil but grows best if it's moist, fertile, and slightly acid. Plant rhizomes in early spring or late summer. Space plants 18 to 24 inches apart. Water to keep moist the first season; after that, the plants are drought tolerant. Divide in spring or late summer when clumps become crowded or start dying out in the center. Less susceptible to disease than bearded iris.

RECOMMENDED VARIETIES: 'Butter and Sugar' stands 2 feet tall with white standards (upright petals) and yellow falls (lower petals). 'Caesar's Brother' is the classic, a 3-foot tall cultivar with dark violet flowers. 'Fourfold White' is a particularly vigorous white-flowering form. 'Super Ego' is a blue and lavender bicolor.

KNAUTIA MACEDONICA

(NAW-tee-uh)

Crimson pincushion

2'

- Eye-catching, 2-inch blossoms all summer
- Excellent cut or dried
- Attracts butterflies

2'

- Zones 4–9 (zone 7 east of the Rocky Mountains)

This somewhat straggly plant is nevertheless charming, with 2-foot-tall, long-lasting deep purple-crimson flower heads "dancing" above low foliage on long, wiry stems. Attractive to bees. Leaves are at the base and ascend the stem.

USES: A lovely addition to the border, the cottage garden, or wild garden. Beautiful floating its open sprays over other lower plants. Try it with other airy bloomers like baby's breath (*Gypsophila*) and *Verbena bonariensis*.

SITING AND CARE: Plant in full sun in well-drained soil. Not terribly tolerant of warm nights. Space plants 18 inches apart. Not usually invasive, but it sometimes self-sows. Remember that it starts out neat and tidy in spring but can become quite floppy. Be sure to deadhead to prevent reseeding and divide clumps if they become crowded.

Crimson pincushion bears clouds of wine-red blossoms on wiry stems.

KNIPHOFIA UVARIA

(nih-FOH-fee-uh)

Torch lily

3'

- Towering flower spikes summer to fall
- Flamboyant colors
- Attracts hummingbirds

3'

- Zones 4–7 (zone 4 with winter protection)

Electric spikes stand 3 to 5 feet tall summer through early fall. Torch lily performs best in warm climates.
USES: A showy accent plant, it's also great for the cut-flower garden. At the back of the border, cool blue bellflower (*Campanula*) covers the coarse, ratty leaves and throws a little water on the "fire."

SITING AND CARE: Plant in full sun in moist, well-drained soil. Avoid windy spots. Space 18 inches apart. After flowering, cut back spent flower stems by half. Division seldom required.

RECOMMENDED VARIETIES: 'Alcazar' bears red flowers with a hint of salmon; it is one of the hardiest and a good rebloomer. 'Earliest of All' blooms with orange-red and yellow flowers several weeks sooner. 'Ice Queen' has creamy-white flowers on 5-foot tall plants. 'Shining Sceptre' grows 3 feet tall with golden tangerine flowers.

'Shining Sceptre' bears 3-foot spikes in flaming gold and tangerine.

LAVATERA THURINGIACA

(lah-vuh-TER-uh)

Tree mallow

5'

- Long summer bloom
- Bushy, gray-green foliage
- Easy to grow
- Zones 6–9 (zone 7

4'

east of the Rocky Mountains)

Tree mallow thrives in heat and humidity. Very showy all summer, it is a shrubby, 4- to 6-foot plant with funnel-shaped pink or white flowers.
USES: Tree mallow is a sizeable plant for a large area, not for small spaces. Plant it with Joe-Pye weed (*Eupatorium*), plume poppy (*Macleaya*), or hollyhocks (*Alcea*) at the back of the border.

SITING AND CARE: Plant in full sun in most areas, afternoon shade in the South. Thrives in moist, well-drained, fertile soil. Space 3 feet apart. Provide ample water. Handpick Japanese beetles, which may become a problem.

RECOMMENDED VARIETIES: 'Barnsley' is a recent introduction that sports fringed white flowers (that fade to pink), each with a contrasting reddish eye, June to frost. 'Bredon Springs' has rich pink flowers with white centers. 'Sense' is a compact (40 inches) and vigorous pink that is hardy to zone 4.

Lavatera 'Barnsley' provides shimmering pink color all summer.

The classic, easy-to-grow shasta daisy is popular and widely available.

LEUCANTHEMUM X SUPERBUM

(loo-KAN-thuh-mum)

Shasta daisy

- Prolific bloomer
- Strong flower stems
- Excellent for cutting
- Zones 5–9

2'
2'

This classic forms attractive clumps of dark-green foliage covered with large daisies 2 or 3 feet tall.
USES: Long-lived and easy, shasta daisy is a staple of cottage gardens. This versatile plant combines well with almost any perennial but makes a particularly lovely partner for daylilies (*Hemerocallis*).
SITING AND CARE: Best in full sun but tolerates partial shade, particularly in hot climates. Provide rich, moist, well-drained soil. Plant 1 foot apart. Remove spent flowers. Mulch for winter protection in cold regions. Be sure to divide every other year in spring.
RECOMMENDED VARIETIES: 'Alaska' is extremely hardy (zone 4) and one of the oldest varieties with pure white flowers. 'Becky' has white, 2-inch-wide flowers that bloom for up to 8 weeks, good heat tolerance, and exceptionally long-lasting foliage. 'Snow Lady' is a compact, 10- to 12-inch dwarf.

'Kobold' blazing star is earlier-blooming and more compact.

LIATRIS SPICATA

(lye-AY-tris)

Blazing star

- Bold flowers, summer to fall
- Superb butterfly plant
- Outstanding cut or dried
- Zones 3–9

3'
2'

A favorite native of prairies and wet meadows, blazing star's bold flowers stand 2 to 5 feet tall.
USES: Unique flowers are beautiful and long lasting, whether in the border or in a vase. Blazing star is suitable for the mixed border and will naturalize in the wildflower garden. Combines well with purple coneflower (*Echinacea*) and lamb's ear (*Stachys*). Attracts bees.
SITING AND CARE: Plant in full sun in well-drained soil. Space 12 to 15 inches apart or sow seeds in spring. Remove spent flowers to promote rebloom. Remember the plants look fine until the flowers are finished. Division seldom needed.
RECOMMENDED VARIETIES AND RELATED SPECIES: 'Kobold' is earliest to bloom with multiple spikes and grows only 24 to 30 inches tall. 'Floristan' is available in both white and purple varieties. *L. scariosa* 'White Spire' has 3-foot-tall white spikes.

LIGULARIA DENTATA

(lig-yew-LARE-ee-uh)

Ligularia

- Cheerful mid to late summer yellows, oranges
- Bold, attractive foliage
- Tall (3 to 6 feet)
- Zones 5–7

3'
3'

Ligularia dentata 'Desdemona' (above) and L. stenocephala 'The Rocket' (right).

Most ligularias stage their best performance in regions with cool nights.
USES: Long-stalked, kidney-shaped leaves provide drama in the garden. Plant with sedges and golden grass (*Hakonechloa*).
SITING AND CARE: Plant in full sun in cool regions; afternoon shade where weather is hot. Soil that is moist but well-drained is essential. Space plants 2 to 3 feet apart. Add organic matter. Water abundantly and feed regularly. (Don't worry if plants in full sun wilt; as long as the soil is moist, they'll recover at sundown.) Division rarely necessary.
RECOMMENDED VARIETIES AND RELATED SPECIES: *L. dentata* 'Desdemona' has reddish orange, daisy-like flowers and deep purple leaves; 'Othello' has orange daisy-like flowers and mahogany red leaves. *L. stenocephala* 'The Rocket' has impressive spikes of bright yellow flowers and purple stems.

LOBELIA CARDINALIS

(loh-BEE-lee-uh)

Cardinal flower

3'
1'

- Brilliant red flowers, midsummer to fall
- Tall and stately
- Good for cutting
- Zones 2–9

Native to wet woods and low meadows, cardinal flower thrives in moist soil. The 3- to 4-foot-tall plants are short-lived but self-sow.
USES: Brilliant splash of red for the late-summer woodland or bog garden. Combine with Siberian or water iris at the edge of the water garden, or pair with rose mallow (*Hibiscus*) or bee balm (*Monarda*) in the border. Attracts hummingbirds.
SITING AND CARE: Plant in partial shade (or in full sun in cool regions with boggy soil). Provide moist, humus-rich, acid soil. Start seed indoors 6 to 8 weeks before planting or sow seed outdoors in late fall or space plants 12 to 18 inches apart in spring. Remove faded flower stalks. Mulch to protect crowns in winter.
RECOMMENDED VARIETIES AND RELATED SPECIES: 'Gladys Lindley' is a creamy white-flowered variety that grows to 4 feet tall. 'Sparkle Divine' has purple-fuschia flowers and a long bloom period.

L. × *speciosa* 'Queen Victoria' has brilliant red flowers over bronze foliage. Great Blue Lobelia (*L. siphilitica*) is a native that grows 2 to 3 feet tall with blue flowers.

Cardinal flower's bright red spires bloom over dark toothy foliage.

LUPINUS 'RUSSELL HYBRID'

(loo-PYE-nus)

Lupine

3'
2'

- Bright June colors and bicolors
- Good cut flower
- Zones 4–6

Impressive but finicky, 30-inch-tall lupine performs best only in light, sandy soil and in locations with cool summers.
USES: Lupine blooms in fabulous showy flowers if you can grow it in your area. They are best massed in beds or combined with hardy geranium or shasta daisy (*Leucanthemum* × *superbum*).
SITING AND CARE: Plant in full sun in cool areas; afternoon shade where it's hot. Provide rich, moist soil with excellent drainage. Space plants 18 to 24 inches apart. Water during dry periods. Mulch in summer to retain moisture and keep roots cool. Mulch in winter only if there is no reliable snow cover.
RECOMMENDED VARIETIES AND RELATED SPECIES: Gallery Hybrids are a dwarf series, 15 to 18 inches tall, blooming in shades of blue, pink, red, and white. 'My Castle' has brick red flowers on 2- to 3-foot-tall plants. 'The Chatelaine' has pink and white bicolor flowers. *L. perennis* is a 24-inch-tall native with blue flowers; hardy in zones 3–7.

The spiky flowers of Russell lupines come in nearly every color.

LYSIMACHIA CLETHROIDES

(liss-ih-MOCK-ee-uh)

Gooseneck loosestrife

3'
3'

- Unique late summer white blossoms
- Vigorous and easy
- Fall color in sun
- Zones 4–6

White spikes arch toward one side on 2- or 3-foot-tall stems. Invasive, especially in moist soil.
USES: Showy blossoms for mass planting. Use alone as a ground cover or combine with blue star (*Amsonia*) or balloon flower (*Platycodon*). Good cut flower.
SITING AND CARE: Plant in full sun or partial shade. Plants make their best growth in moist, humus-rich soil. Plant 15 to 24 inches apart. Divide in spring as necessary to restrain the size of the clump.
RELATED SPECIES: Yellow loosestrife (*L. punctata*) blooms in bright-yellow whorls around each individual flower stalk.

A patch of gooseneck loosestrife in bloom resembles a flock of geese.

Yellow loosestrife is fond of moist, shady areas and may be invasive.

LYTHRUM SALICARIA

(LIH-thrum)
Purple loosestrife

- Spectacular blooms, summer to fall
- Indestructible
- Vertical accent
- Good for cutting
- Zones 3–9

Purple loosestrife crowds out native wetland species, so plant with care.

Unfortunately this bushy, 3- to 5-foot plant is invasive in wet soils, and is choking waterways in many regions. In some states, purple loosestrife is a noxious weed and is illegal to grow, particularly in the Northwest, Northeast, West, and Midwest. Hybrid varieties may be less rampant. Check with your county cooperative extension agent. **USES:** A spectacular, long-blooming perennial for areas away from waterways, even where legal. Combine with ornamental grasses for a beautiful and easy-care border. **SITING AND CARE:** Plant in sun or partial shade in average to dry soil to curtail invasive nature. Space plants 24 inches apart. Plants are tolerant of heat and humidity and do well in southern gardens as long as enough moisture is provided. Remove spent blossoms to promote continued blooms and prevent self-sowing. Division of woody roots is difficult and seldom necessary. **RECOMMENDED VARIETIES AND RELATED SPECIES:** 'Firecandle' ('Feuerkerze') has rose-red plumes. *L. virgatum* 'Morden's Pink' has rose-pink plumes.

Plume poppy's creamy white flowers top gigantic yet graceful plants.

MACLEAYA CORDATA

(ma-KLAY-uh)
Plume poppy

- Creamy early summer plumes
- Hairy, heart-shaped leaves
- Sturdy and heat tolerant
- Zones 3–8

This huge plant, 6 to 10 feet tall, with its 10- to 12-inch airy plumes, is invasive in almost all areas, particularly if soil is rich and moist. It requires plenty of room. **USES:** Impressive plant for large gardens. Use as a living screen, or plant at the back of an expansive border (or center of an island bed) with Joe-Pye weed (*Eupatorium*) or rodgersia. **SITING AND CARE:** Plant in full sun or partial shade. Allow 6 feet between plants. Install a barrier to keep roots from spreading beyond allotted area, if necessary. Divide every two years or as necessary to reduce crowded clumps. **RECOMMENDED VARIETIES AND RELATED SPECIES:** 'Flamingo' is a pink-flowered variety on gray-green stems. *M. microcarpa* 'Coral Plume' is similar to *M. cordata*, 8 feet tall with showy coral-pink blooms.

MALVA ALCEA

(MAL-va)
Hollyhock mallow

- Summer-to-frost flowers
- Drought tolerant
- Sturdy stems
- Zones 4–7

Hollyhock mallow is best in full sun.

This free-flowering plant is tall (3 or 4 feet) and bushy with heart-shaped, scalloped leaves and funnel-shaped purplish pink flowers. Hollyhock mallow is prone to problems in hot, humid areas. **USES:** Easy and handsome plant that brightens the garden for most of the summer. Use as a summer hedge, or plant in combination with obedient plant (*Physotegia*) or balloon flower (*Platycodon*). **SITING AND CARE:** Plant in any well-drained soil in full sun in most areas; partial shade in the South. Space plants 18 inches apart or sow seeds in spring. Cut back top 12 inches after first flush to promote continued blossoming. Handpick Japanese beetles as necessary. Division isn't necessary because plants are short-lived. **RECOMMENDED VARIETIES AND RELATED SPECIES:** 'Fastigiata' produces attractive deep pink flowers well into autumn and has a neater form. *M. sylvestris* 'Zebrina' has strong, erect stems and white to pink flowers with raspberry red markings. The flowers resemble pinwheels throughout the summer. Hardy to zone 5.

MATTEUCCIA STRUTHIOPTERIS

(mah-TOO-chee-uh)

Ostrich fern

5'

- Vase-shaped
- Big and bold
- Rapid spreader
- Zones 2–7

3'

Unsurpassed for its perfect, dramatic fronds that resemble ostrich feathers; it grow 4 to 6 feet tall.

USES: If you want the classic fern look in a grouping, this vigorous fern is your choice. It is great for naturalizing in dappled shade.

SITING AND CARE: Best in shade but tolerates sun if soil never dries out. Grows well in average to moist soil. Plant 3 feet apart. Water if dry to prevent leaf scorch. Does not do well in the hot summers of the South. Fiddleheads are edible.

Ostrich fern can reach 6 feet tall.

MISCANTHUS SINENSIS

(miss-KAN-thus)

Maiden grass

8'

- Large pink or silver fall plumes
- Winter interest
- Tall and narrow
- Zones 6–9

3'

This outstanding grass—valued for its foliage and flowers—forms dense clumps that grow 6 to 12 feet tall.

USES: The fall flowers of maiden grass begin as drooping purple-tinged fans. These open to long, silky spikelets that mature in late summer to dazzling plumes of silvery hairs that last well into winter. It is beautiful as a backdrop for monkshood (*Aconitum*) or rodgersia.

SITING AND CARE: Plant in full sun (flops in shade) in average to heavy soil. Moderate to wet conditions; drought tolerant. Allow 4 to 5 feet between plants.

RECOMMENDED VARIETIES AND RELATED SPECIES: 'Gracillimus' grows 3 to 4 feet tall with silvery plumes and narrow, curly leaves. Flame grass ('Purpurascens') has orange-red fall color and silvery plumes. 'Morning Light' has white-striped leaves and flower stems to 6 feet. 'Silver Feather' has silvery white flowers high above the foliage. Porcupine grass ('Strictus') has yellow striping on vertical leaves and stands more erect than zebra grass ('Zebrinus').

Flame grass ('Purpurascens') turns salmon, pink, or gold in part shade.

'Morning Light' appears gray-green.

Maiden grass makes an excellent backdrop for Rudbeckia 'Goldsturm'.

MOLINIA CAERULEA 'VARIEGATA'

(moh-LEE-ni-uh)

Purple moor grass

18"

- Purplish pink flowers
- Forms dense tufts
- Deciduous
- Zones 4–9

18"

Native to acid moorlands, this graceful ornamental grass stands 18 inches tall in flower.

USES: This is one of the most popular garden grasses because of its elegant habit and fall beauty. Use it as a ground cover or a specimen.

SITING AND CARE: Plant in full sun in acid to neutral, moderately moist soil. Space 2 feet apart.

RELATED SPECIES: Tall purple moor grass (*M. caerulea arundinacea*), has fine-textured foliage only 2 to 3 feet tall, but the flowers appearing high above arch out 7 to 8 feet high (they make a marvelous gauzy screen in front of a window); 'Skyracer' is 7 to 8 feet tall with more erect stems, and good yellow-orange fall color.

Purple moor grass produces purple spikelets on yellow-tinted stems.

MONARDA DIDYMA

(moh-NAR-da)

Bee balm

Bee balm 'Cambridge Scarlet' has red flowers and is mildew resistant.

30"

18"

- Fluffy blossoms, late spring to fall
- Mint-scented leaves
- Excellent cut flower
- Zones 3-8

This dense, lush, 2- to 3-foot plant spreads rapidly. Originally red, colors now include salmon, pink, white, purple, and burgundy.

USES: Bee balm is one of the best for attracting hummingbirds and butterflies, but it can be invasive.

SITING AND CARE: Plant in full sun or partial shade in moist, humus-rich soil. Space 24 inches apart. Water abundantly, but withhold fertilizer and thin regularly to restrict spreading. Divide every

two years. In humid climates, mildew is often troublesome.

RECOMMENDED VARIETIES AND RELATED SPECIES: 'Gardenview Scarlet' has red blossoms, mildew-resistant leaves. 'Marshall's Delight' is hot pink with disease-resistant foliage. 'Petite Delight' is a foot-tall, mildew-resistant dwarf with rosy pink flowers. 'Jacob Kline' is a 48-inch variety with large deep red flowers, noted for mildew resistance. 'Mahogany' is a dark wine-red-flowered form with good disease resistance. Wild bergamot (M. *fistulosa*) is a native prairie plant that grows 2 to 5 feet tall with lavender flowers.

NEPETA X FAASSENII

(NEH-peh-tuh)

Catmint

18"

18"

- Cool blue summer-long blossoms
- Fragrant foliage
- Trouble-free ground cover
- Zones 3–8 (zone 7 east of the Rocky Mountains)

The bushy, aromatic, gray-green foliage appeals to people as much as cats. An important source of blue for the front of the border, catmint produces billowing masses of small flowers for several weeks. One to 3 feet tall, depending on variety.

Catmint's profuse spikes of cool blue-lavender blossom all summer.

USES: Its beautiful blue tapestry weaves together other perennials. A classic edging for rose gardens, use catmint to border formal flower and herb gardens. For a dandy partner, try 'Moonbeam' threadleaf coreopsis, or pair with bearded iris.

SITING AND CARE: Plant in full sun in well-drained soil. Space 18 inches apart. Shear after first flush of flowers. Divide in spring or fall every three years.

RECOMMENDED VARIETIES: 'Blue Wonder' is a 12- to 15-inch ground cover with 6-inch blue spikes. 'Six Hills Giant' is a tall form with dark violet flowers. 'White Wonder' is a white-flowering form of 'Blue Wonder'.

OSMUNDA CINNAMOMEA

(oz-MOON-da)

Cinnamon fern

36"

18"

- Robust
- Elegant form
- Sun tolerant
- Zones 3–7

Cinnamon fern's erect center fronds look like cinnamon sticks in spring.

Royal fern tolerates some sun, where it achieves the best fall color (inset).

Cinnamon fern grows 3 feet or more in moist soil, good for cool areas.

USES: This is a good choice for a sunny, low-lying spot. It is ideal for planting where water stands, and at the water's edge.

SITING AND CARE: Plant in light shade or full sun in constantly moist, acid soil. Space 2 feet apart. Be sure not to allow soil to dry out.

RELATED SPECIES: Royal fern (O. *regalis*) is typically 4 to 6 feet tall, but can grow up to 9 feet in wet areas, and is one of the largest garden ferns. It's fairly sun tolerant if it receives good moisture.

PAEONIA HYBRIDS

(pee-OH-nee-uh)

Peony

3'

■ Fragrant, late-spring blossoms
■ Long-lived plants
■ Superb cut flowers
■ Zones 3-8

Beyond its famous late-spring flowers, this bushy, 3-foot plant is attractive all summer, and even into autumn with its red-tinged foliage.

USES: A stalwart of the perennial garden, peony provides beauty for a lifetime. Substantial plants can easily stand alone but look grand surrounded with low-growing, fine-textured perennials. Good companions are blue star (*Amsonia*) and false indigo (*Baptisia*).

SITING AND CARE: Plant in full sun to partial shade in well-drained soil enriched with compost. Plant in late summer or early fall, with eyes (pinkish buds on top of the root) 1 to 2 inches below the soil surface. Space 3 feet apart. Provide support before bloom time. Remove all foliage after frost in fall. Division, while best done in fall, is rarely necessary and not advised. Thrives in cold-winter climates.

RECOMMENDED VARIETIES: A lifetime could be spent collecting peonies. A few of the classics: 'Festiva Maxima' is a double white with red flecks at the base of petals. 'Kansas' is an award-winning bright red double. 'Krinkled White' bears single snow white flowers with yellow stamens. 'Sarah Bernhardt' is a double pink with silvery edges.

Spring blossoms come in an intriguing variety of colors, such as 'White Cheddar' (here with larkspur).

'West Elkton' petals are slightly crinkled and surround a mass of unusual yellow stamens.

'Gay Paree' has a "bomb" flower form with brilliant magenta petals and a peach-pink center.

Large, fluffy apple-blossom pink flowers of 'Sarah Bernhardt'.

Paeonia tenuifolia 'Flora Plena' bears red flowers atop ferny foliage.

The deep fuchsia-purple 'Kansas' is marbled on the outside.

Paeonia mlokosewitschii 'Molly the Witch' has primrose yellow flowers.

'Duchesse de Nemours' is a creamy white "bomb" tinted yellow.

'Largo' has rose-pink petals surrounding pink and gold centers.

PANICUM VIRGATUM

(PAN-i-kum)

Switch grass

- Airy fall flowers
- Autumn color
- Persistent through winter
- Zones 3–9

'Heavy Metal' switch grass has blue-green leaves and an upright form.

Switch grass puts on a lovely autumn show.

Switch grass is a vigorous, 5-foot-tall native prairie plant that does well in seaside gardens. **USES:** One of the most fine-textured of the tall grasses, it is beautiful as a specimen or nice as a living screen. Flowers are excellent for cutting or drying.

SITING AND CARE: Best in full sun and in light, sandy, moist soil. Space 3 feet apart.

RECOMMENDED VARIETIES: 'Cloud Nine' is 6 feet tall with seed heads looking like clouds above the foliage. 'Haense Herms' grows 3 to 4 feet tall, with red fall color. 'Heavy Metal' has upright, metallic-blue leaves, turning amber-yellow in fall and beige in winter. Red switch grass ('Rotstrahlbusch') is considered the reddest variety. It grows to 3 feet tall, then to 4 feet with flowers. Tall switch grass ('Strictum') has blue leaves and eventually reaches 5 or 6 feet tall.

Large, vibrant, crepe-paperlike blossoms make 'Salmon Glow' a most popular poppy.

PAPAVER ORIENTALE

(puh-PAH-ver)

Oriental poppy

- Bright spring colors
- Old-fashioned favorite
- Good for cutting
- Zones 2–7

Oriental poppy varieties have red, orange, pink, or white blossoms, often with dark centers. This coarse-leaved plant, 2 to 4 feet tall, is not tolerant of heat and humidity. **USES:** One of the most loved and beautiful of flowers, it's an excellent choice for the cottage garden.

SITING AND CARE: Plant in full sun in well-drained soil. Plant dormant crowns 3 inches below soil level in late summer, or container plants in spring, spaced 15 to 20 inches apart. Stake plants with tall stems. Divide every four years in late summer. Foliage dies back after flowering and remains dormant.

RECOMMENDED VARIETIES: 'Black and White' produces white petals with black spots at the base. 'Brilliant' blooms fire-engine red on 30-inch plants. 'Helen Elizabeth' is a classic with salmon pink flowers. 'Maiden's Blush' has ruffled white-and-pink blooms on 3-foot plants. 'Raspberry Queen' has huge dark pink flowers on 3-foot plants.

Golden lace's airy clusters of brilliant yellow blossoms light up the garden.

PATRINIA SCABIOSIFOLIA

(pa-TRIN-ee-uh)

Golden lace

- Long summer to fall season of flowers
- Easy to grow
- Good for cut flowers
- Zones 5–8

You can count on this 3- to 5-foot plant to bloom with yellow cup-shaped flowers from summer to fall. It goes well with just about everything in the garden. **USES:** This seldom-used perennial blends beautifully with other mid- to late-summer flowers. Grow in a woodland or rock garden or in a mixed border. Try pairing it with purple coneflower (*Echinacea*) or globe thistle (*Echinops*). Excellent with *Verbena bonariensis* and Russian sage (*Perovskia*).

SITING AND CARE: Plant in full sun to partial shade in dry, well-drained soil. Space 18 to 24 inches apart. Division is not necessary. It often reseeds, enough to be a pleasure not a problem.

RECOMMENDED VARIETIES AND RELATED SPECIES: 'Nagoya' is a compact version, 24 to 36 inches tall. *P. triloba* forms 12-inch-tall mounds of foliage from which clusters of small sulfur yellow flowers bloom on wiry stems.

PENNISETUM ALOPECUROIDES

(pen-ih-SEE-tum)

Perennial fountain grass

3'
- Narrow leaves
- Arching, copper flowers
- Yellow fall color
- Zones 5–9

2'

Fine-textured, glossy green leaves form a dense mass that remains green into fall, then changes to rose, apricot, or gold before bleaching almond for winter.

USES: One of the most useful grasses for the flower garden and mixed borders. Robust and beautiful, 3-foot-tall fountain grass combines attractively with black-eyed Susan (*Rudbeckia*).
SITING AND CARE: Grow in full sun in the North (full sun to light shade in the South) and moist, well-drained, fertile soil. Be sure to plant 3 feet apart.
RECOMMENDED VARIETIES: 'Hameln' is smaller and finer than the species fountain grass, and grows to 2 feet tall and wide. 'Little Bunny' is very short, good for rock gardens. 'Moudry' grows 30 inches tall with deep green leaves and black flower plumes in fall.

Fountain grass forms attractive seed heads earlier than most grasses.

PENSTEMON

(PEN-steh-mon)

Beard-tongue

30"
- Early summer show
- Great for cutting
- Tubular flowers in brilliant colors

18"
- Zones 2–9 (zone 2 east of the Rocky Mountains)

Beard-tongues include spectacular western wildflowers, as well as species suitable for the garden, even in hot, humid regions.
USES: This showy flower comes in a wide range of colors and is a good choice for wildflower meadows.

Or plant it in the border along with other perennials that like similar conditions, like fleabane (*Erigeron*).
SITING AND CARE: Plant in full sun or partial shade in light, well-drained soil. Where marginally hardy, protect in winter. Sow seeds or space plants 1 to 2 feet apart, depending on mature width. Mulch lightly in winter in cold areas.
RECOMMENDED VARIETIES AND RELATED SPECIES: *P. barbatus* 'Prairie Fire' is a scarlet variety for zones 4 to 8. *P. digitalis* 'Husker Red' has red leaves throughout spring and fall, white summer blossoms. Zones 3 to 8. 'Midnight' with deep purple flowers is best for the South; zones 6 to 8.

Penstemon barbatus (left) and 'Margery Fish' (right).

PEROVSKIA ATRIPLICIFOLIA

(puh-ROFF-skee-uh)

Russian sage

4'
- Aromatic blooms, summer to fall
- Handsome, bushy plants

3'
- Tolerates drought and heat
- Zones 2–9

Valued for late-season effect, this long-blooming, aromatic, 3- to 4-foot perennial begins its show of two-lipped, lavender-blue flowers in midsummer and carries on into fall. Easy to grow in all climates.

USES: Russian sage creates a silvery effect combined with grasses and other large-scale perennials in informal settings. It is a wonderful background plant for black-eyed Susan (*Rudbeckia*) or phlox.
SITING AND CARE: Plant in full sun in well-drained soil. Space plants 3 feet apart. Cut back to the ground after frost.
RECOMMENDED VARIETIES: 'Blue Spire' grows 36 inches tall with finely-dissected leaves. 'Filagran' has light blue flowers and filagreed foliage, giving it a more delicate appearance than other varieties. Narrow and upright 'Longin' is 4 feet tall with deep violet-blue flowers on erect stems.

The foliage of Russian sage releases a sagelike scent when crushed.

PHLOX PANICULATA

(flocks pah-nih-kew-LAY-tuh)

Garden phlox

- Marvelous summer-long fragrance
- Grand for cutting
- Old-fashioned favorite
- Zones 4–8

Garden phlox's spectacular clusters bloom for weeks in summer.

Also called summer phlox, its blossoms come in shades of pink, red, purple, and white.

USES: Garden phlox is unexcelled for color and fragrance and is superb in cottage garden borders with globe thistle (*Echinops*) or hollyhock mallow (*Malva*).

SITING AND CARE: Plant in full sun or partial shade in evenly moist, rich, well-drained soil. Space 24 inches apart. Thin clumps to three to five shoots per plant to provide good air circulation and to control mildew. Water abundantly in dry weather. Subject to mildew in humid climates; fungicide is often required for all but mildew-resistant varieties. Cut spent blooms for best rebloom. May need division every three years.

RECOMMENDED VARIETIES AND RELATED SPECIES: 'David' is pure white and mildew resistant. 'Eva Cullum' is bright pink with a red eye. It is disease resistant, as is 'Robert Poore', a purple. 'Starfire' is the truest red variety. Woodland phlox (*Phlox divaricata*) is a good blue for shade, only 8 inches high.

PHLOX SUBULATA

(flocks sub-yoo-LAH-tuh)

Creeping phlox

- Bright, clear spring colors
- Moss-like foliage
- Evergreen mats
- Zones 2–8

Creeping phlox may be pink, lavender, blue, or white with yellow eyes.

Creeping phlox is a magnificent low ground cover that blooms lavishly in sunny gardens from early to midspring. When they bloom, these creepers (6 to 8 inches tall) are covered with a mass of pink, red, white, or lavender.

USES: Creeping phlox is ideal as a ground cover or planted around shrubs. Makes a pretty edging and pairs well with daffodils. This is the most fragrant of the phloxes.

SITING AND CARE: Plant in full sun in well-drained, light, neutral to alkaline soil. Plant clumps a foot apart. Thin out whenever clumps become crowded. Mulch lightly to protect its shallow roots but avoid smothering the evergreen leaves.

RECOMMENDED VARIETIES: 'Candy Stripe' has white flowers striped with pink. 'Emerald Gem' is a light pink with a mounding habit. 'Scarlet Flame' is deep red. 'Red Wings' is a heavy-blooming rosy red. 'Snowflake' is the showiest white variety.

PHORMIUM TENAX

(FOR-mee-um)

New Zealand flax

- Midsummer flowers
- Bold, colorful leaves
- Evergreen
- Zones 8–10

New Zealand flax 'Sundowner' has rusty bronze, leathery, swordlike leaves.

Native to the swamps of New Zealand, this flax grows 5 to 7 feet tall in clumps and ranges from yellow-green to dark green, with many fine stripes.

USES: Grown for dramatic effect and colorful foliage, New Zealand flax has limited adaptability but is great as an annual in the North. It is perfect for planting at the edge of a water garden, as a focal point in the border, or in a container.

SITING AND CARE: Grow in full sun in deep, fertile, moist soil. Plant in a sheltered spot. Water to keep soil moist.

RECOMMENDED VARIETIES AND RELATED SPECIES: 'Aurora' bears leaves striped with red, pink, and yellow. 'Burgundy' is a deep wine red. 'Purpureum' has a purple-red sheen to its leaves. 'Williamsii Variegated' has wide yellow-veined green leaves. Mountain flax (*P. colensoi* and *cookianum*) is a smaller, 3-foot plant with pendulous flowers. Numerous useful varieties exist.

PHYSOSTEGIA VIRGINIANA

(fye-soh-STEE-jee-uh)

Obedient plant

3'
2'

■ **Pink or white snapdragon-like spikes**
■ **Excellent for cutting**
■ **Easy and vigorous**
■ **Zones 2–9**

This slender 2- or 3-foot plant is hardy throughout the country and is a good choice for seaside gardens and cut flowers.
USES: Beautiful but rampant and invasive, it's ideal for poor soils. Excellent for late-summer color in borders and naturalistic gardens.

Naturalize in a wildflower garden or plant in the border with shasta daisy (*Leucanthemum × superbum*).
SITING AND CARE: Grow in full sun to partial shade in lean to average soil. Space 18 inches apart. Provide moderate to plentiful moisture. Stake taller varieties when grown in fertile soil or in shade. Divide clumps in the border every year or two to restrain growth.
RECOMMENDED VARIETIES: Early-blooming 'Summer Snow' has white flowers and is slower to spread than most. 'Variegata' blooms pink, with beautiful white markings on green leaves. 'Vivid' has a dwarf habit; it is 20 inches tall with bright orchid pink blossoms.

Obedient plant's flowers will stay in place when bent on the stalk.

PHYTOLACCA AMERICANA

(fye-toh-LAH-ka)

Pokeweed

6'
4'

■ **White flower spikes, summer to fall**
■ **Tall and bold**
■ **Poisonous berries**
■ **Zones 4–9**

This 6-foot-tall plant is an eastern native of damp thickets and open woodlands. Traditionally harvested for its young leaves, Pokeweed has been relegated to weed status in most of the U. S. However, some gardeners appreciate the plant for its bold color, size, and form, and its

ornamental use is gaining favor. Midsummer to early autumn it bears white to pink flowers. But in fall, it's screaming red stems and glossy black berries are simply gorgeous.
USES: Pokeweed is an expansive plant for large gardens or for naturalizing in woodland gardens.
SITING AND CARE: Plant in sun or partial shade in lean, moist soil. Plant seeds or space plants 2 or 3 feet apart. Support taller species in open sites.
RELATED SPECIES: Chinese poke (*P. clavigera*) has oval green leaves with white midribs and long trusses of pink flowers. Less aggressive and tidier than *P. americana*, this species is probably hardy to zone 6.

Pokeweed's reddish stems and shiny black berries make a pretty contrast.

PLATYCODON GRANDIFLORUS

(pla-ti-KOH-don)

Balloon flower

36"
18"

■ **Bell-shaped blossoms early to midsummer**
■ **Excellent for cutting**
■ **Reliable and long-lived**
■ **Zones 3–7**

Pink, white, or blue balloon flower is a real child pleaser, with its 2-foot plants and inflated flower buds.
USES: Elegant blooms of these fun and easy plants blend beautifully with almost any other flower.

Excellent for summer gardens, this plant combines well with daylilies (*Hemerocallis*) and lilies.
SITING AND CARE: Plant in full sun in most areas, partial shade in warmest regions, in well-drained soil. Space plants 18 inches apart. Remove spent flowers to promote rebloom. Stake tall varieties. Mark location; plants are late to emerge in spring. No need to divide.
RECOMMENDED VARIETIES: 'Albus' is a white form with bluish veins. 'Mariesii' has blue-violet flowers and a compact, 15-inch size. 'Sentimental Blue' has 2-inch flowers on 8-inch dwarf plants. 'Shell Pink' is a soft shell pink, 18 to 24 inches tall.

The unique buds of balloon flower look like puffy blue balloons.

POLYGONATUM ODORATUM 'VARIEGATUM'

(poh-lih-go-NAY-tum)

Variegated Solomon's seal

■ Fragrant
■ Lovely in every season
■ Tolerates dry shade
■ Elegant arching stems
■ Zones 4–9 (zone 8 east of the Rocky Mountains)

Solomon's seal's arching foliage is an asset to the dry shade garden.

Yellow fall foliage of Solomon's seal illuminates the autumn woodland.

Flowers are soon followed by black berries, but it's the 2-foot white-and-green varigated arching foliage for which this plant is mostly prized. The leaves turn yellow in fall.
USES: Its interesting form adds variety to the woodland garden. It is an ideal companion for hosta, toad lily (*Tricyrtus*), and ferns.
SITING AND CARE: Tolerates dry shade but best in light shade and rich, moist soil. Space 1 foot apart.
RELATED SPECIES: Great Solomon's seal (*P. commutatum*) grows twice as big (5 to 7 feet high), with blue-green leaves. Dwarf Solomon's seal (*P. humile*) is a miniature version growing 6 to 10 inches tall. Zones 3 to 9.

POLYSTICHUM ACROSTICHOIDES

(poh-LISS-ti-kum)

Christmas fern

■ Evergreen foliage
■ Spreads slowly
■ Good for cutting
■ Zones 4–8

Christmas fern is native and common to eastern North America.

Western sword fern.

Bushy, 2-foot-tall ferns look something like the Boston fern that is grown indoors.
USES: This attractive fern combines well with many woodland perennials and is beautiful with bergenia or corydalis. Cut fronds are popular for Christmas decorations, thus its name.
SITING AND CARE: Plant in partial shade in moist but well-drained, acid or neutral soil. Space 18 inches apart. Water in dry weather. This fern is tough and undemanding.
RELATED SPECIES: Western sword fern (*P. munitum*) produces beautiful, large clumps of deep green fronds. Hardy only to zone 7, it is an important landscape plant for the coastal western U.S. Tassel fern (*P. polyblepharum*) is a handsome fern with evergreen, glossy, dark green fronds, 24 inches tall.

PRIMULA JAPONICA

(PRIM-yew-la ja-PON-ih-kuh)

Japanese primrose

■ Cheerful, rainbow of early spring color
■ Prolific bloomer
■ Handsome foliage
■ Zones 5–9 (varies with variety)

Candelabra primrose 'Inshriach' ranges from orange through purple.

Japanese primrose 'Redfield Strain' is a must for the moist woodland.

There are hundreds of primroses, some easy, some difficult, ranging from a few inches to 3 feet tall.
USES: Primrose is a favorite for its early flowers in the woodland.
SITING AND CARE: Plant in filtered shade under high branches in rich, deep, moist, well-drained soil high in organic matter. Good bog plant. Water abundantly during dry spells. Mulch. Trap slugs and snails. Plants may go dormant in summer and reappear in fall. Divide every third year after flowering.
RELATED SPECIES: Candelabra primroses are a complex group of hybrids with tall, multi-tiered spikes in shades of orange, red, purple and pink, excellent for bog gardens.

PRIMULA VULGARIS

(PRIM-yew-la vul-GARE-iss)

English primrose

6"
8"

- Tubular, sulfur-yellow blossoms in spring
- Semi-evergreen leaves
- Zones 4–8

This easy-to-grow primrose is the best species for southern gardens. Deep-veined leaves grow in rosettes from which the flowers emerge on 8-inch stems.
USES: Good for massing in moist woodland settings.
SITING AND CARE: Grow in partial shade and well-drained soils. Tolerates full sun if soil remains continually moist. Fall planting for winter bloom in mild-winter areas.

RELATED SPECIES: *P. vialii* produces spikes of intense blue-violet flowers on leafless stems late in the spring. Performs well in the West.

A favorite springtime florist plant, English primrose produces short-stemmed, pale yellow flowers.

Looking nothing like its cousins, P. vialii bears spikes of red buds that open into violet-purple flowers.

PULMONARIA SACCHARATA

(pul-moh-NARE-ee-uh)

Bethlehem sage

1'
2'

- Pink buds, blue spring flowers
- Beautiful foliage
- Easy and long-lived in shade
- Zone 3–7

Flowers bloom in spring, but the slow-growing clumps of low foliage (about 1 foot tall) remain attractive throughout the season.
USES: Its attractive, speckled foliage makes a pretty ground cover for shade. Plant at the front of a shady border with spring bulbs.
SITING AND CARE: Plant in full or partial shade in moist, humus-rich soil. Space 10 inches apart. Control slugs and snails. Water in dry periods to keep leaves lush. (Established plants are drought tolerant, but leaves will brown. Remove tattered leaves and new ones will soon take their place.)
RECOMMENDED VARIETIES AND RELATED SPECIES: 'Excalibur' bears rosy flowers and silver leaves edged in green. 'Mrs. Moon' has dark green foliage with silver polka dots. *P. longifolia* 'Bertram Anderson' has violet-blue flowers; 'Roy Davidson' has wonderfully silver-dappled, lancelike leaves.

White speckles on dark green leaves of 'Roy Davidson' (above) and the lovely blossoms of 'Mrs. Moon' (right) rise above spotted foliage.

RHEUM PALMATUM

(REE-um)

Chinese rhubarb

7'
5'

- Tall red summer spikes
- Massive, fan-shaped leaves
- Colorful stems and interesting foliage
- Zones 5–7

This ornamental grows just like the rhubarb in the food garden, but it's prettier—and bigger, 6 to 8 feet tall and nearly as wide.
USES: With its 2- to 3-foot-wide leaves, this rhubarb is quite imposing and is perfect as an accent, especially at water's edge. Or pair it with fine-textured perennials like astilbe.
SITING AND CARE: Plant in full sun or partial shade in fertile, well-drained, moist soil. Space 5 feet apart. Spade in compost or other organic matter before planting and topdress with more each spring. Supply ample water in dry weather and mulch to conserve moisture. Division isn't necessary unless performance declines.
RECOMMENDED VARIETIES: 'Atrosanguineum' has emerging red leaves that gradually turn purple, red stems, and a huge stalk topped with a pinkish red plume.

R. tanguticum produces fan-shaped leaves of rich purple. Flower color varies between white, pink, and red.

Rhubarb 'Buckwheat' is massive.

RODGERSIA PINNATA

(rod-JER-zee-uh)

Rodgersia

Rodgersia *'Superba' has handsome foliage with clusters of pink flowers.*

The new growth of Rodgersia podophylla rubra *is a striking red.*

- Astilbe-like, early-summer blossoms
- Big and bold
- Bronze-purple leaves
- Shade or bog gardens
- Zones 5–7

In early summer, plumes rise above umbrella leaves of 4-foot-tall plants.
USES: Rodgersia is a spectacular plant for boggy areas and pairs well with Joe-Pye weed (*Eupatorium*).
SITING AND CARE: Plant in partial shade and moist soil near water's edge. Space 3 feet apart. Water to keep soil constantly moist.
RECOMMENDED VARIETIES AND RELATED SPECIES: 'Superba' has rosy red flowers. *R. aesculifolia* has leaves with a bronze tint and deep decorative veins. *R. podophylla* has creamy white flowers and bronze-red leaves. *R. sambucifolia* grows only 3 feet tall. Its flowers are creamy white.

RUDBECKIA FULGIDA

(rood-BEK-ee-uh)

Black-eyed Susan

Neon-yellow *'Goldsturm' black-eyed Susan blooms late summer into fall.*

- Bold color, late summer to fall
- Great for cutting
- Rugged and dependable
- Zones 3–8

Handsome foliage adds to the show of these beloved native wildflowers. Plants grow 2 or 3 feet tall.
USES: Rudbeckia puts on a sensational end-of-summer show. It is perfect for the wildflower meadow, or pair with aster or Russian sage (*Perovskia*) in the sunny mixed border.
SITING AND CARE: Plant in full sun in fertile, well-drained soil. Space 12 to 24 inches apart.

Drought tolerant once established. Divide every four or five years to maintain vigor. Allow dried seed heads to remain in winter.
RECOMMENDED VARIETIES AND RELATED SPECIES: 'Goldsturm' has golden yellow flowers, lovely, compact, dark green leaves, and is just about everyone's vote for best performer. *R. nitida* 'Herbsonne' grows 5 feet tall with drooping sulfur yellow flowers highlighted with green cones. Cutleaf coneflower (*R. laciniata* 'Goldquelle') has 3-inch gold, double, ruffled flowers. *R. maxima* is a southern wildflower with huge black cones and bright yellow petals on plants 5 feet tall or more.

SALVIA X SYLVESTRIS

(SAL-vee-ah)

Sage

Deep indigo blue 'May Night' is a dependable, early-blooming sage.

- Long summer blooming
- Heat tolerant
- Easy to grow
- Zones 4–8

A wonderful and large group of plants, some are grown for their eye-catching flower spikes, others for their attractive and fragrant foliage.
USES: These dependable plants put on superb garden performance. They are wonderful for the rock garden, with its excellent drainage.
SITING AND CARE: Plant in full sun in well-drained soil. Space 15 to 36 inches apart, depending on variety. Remove spent blossoms to encourage rebloom.

RECOMMENDED VARIETIES AND RELATED SPECIES: 'Blue Hill' (*S. x sylvestris* 'Blauhügel') is a long-flowering blue variety, hardy to zone 4. 'East Friesland' ('Ostfriesland') forms neat, compact mounds with violet-purple flowers; zone 4. 'May Night' ('Mainacht') has deep indigo purple flowers on compact, 18-inch plants; zone 4. *S. verticillata* 'Purple Rain' has arching stems with small purple flowers; zone 4. Silver sage (*S. argenta*) is a biennial grown mainly for its large, wooly leaves, 2 to 4 feet tall; zone 5. *S. officinalis* 'Aurea' is a compact variety of common sage with striking gold and green leaves. It tolerates heat and humidity better than most; zone 6.

SCABIOSA CAUCASICA

(skay-bee-OH-sa)

Pincushion flower

24"
18"

- Blooms all summer
- Butterfly favorite
- Perfect for cutting
- Zones 3–7

Long-stemmed blossoms dance over low mounds of gray-green foliage. **USES:** Pincushion flower provides a beautiful accent in a mixed border. Plant in groups in front of cottage, rock, and informal gardens. For a smashing flower show all summer, grow it in drifts with threadleaf coreopsis 'Moonbeam'. **SITING AND CARE:** Plant in full sun, well-drained soil. Space 12 inches apart. Mulch, and water in dry weather. Deadhead to prolong blooming. Divide in spring if clumps start to degenerate.
RECOMMENDED VARIETIES AND RELATED SPECIES: 'Alba' has large pure white flowers, which are good for cutting. 'Fama' has numerous, large, lavender-blue flowers with silver centers and grows 18 inches tall. *S. columbaria* 'Butterfly Blue' is an exceptionally long-blooming blue, 12 inches tall;

'Pink Mist' is a similar long-blooming variety in lavender-pink.

Scabiosa 'Butterfly Blue' is valued for its long-blooming blue flowers.

SEDUM SPECTABILE

(SEE-dum)

Stonecrop

24"
18"

- Flat-topped flowers bloom summer to frost
- Fall and winter interest
- Easy and long-lived
- Zones 3–10 (zone 8 east of the Rocky Mountains)

This is one of the most popular perennials for its foolproof nature and extraordinarily long season of effect. Botanists are currently changing its name to *Hylotelephium*. **USES:** A summer-to-winter highlight in borders and ideal for rock gardens. Attracts butterflies. **SITING AND CARE:** Plant in well-drained soil in full sun, partial shade in warmer regions. It's wonderful with daylilies (*Hemerocallis*) or grasses. Space 12 to 18 inches apart. Pinch back new growth in spring, if desired, to make plants shorter and increase flowers. If clumps become crowded, divide in spring.
RECOMMENDED VARIETIES AND RELATED SPECIES: 'Autumn Joy' has rosy-pink flowers turning to bronze, on 18-inch, blue-green plants. 'Brilliant' is similar but shorter and blooms earlier. 'Meteor' is 15 inches tall with carmine red flowers. 'Ruby Glow' has sprawling, 10-inch-tall stems with ruby flowers. *Sedum* 'Vera Jameson' has mahogany foliage 10 to 12 inches tall and dusky-pink flowers. *S. kamtschaticum* 'Weihenstephaner Gold' makes a lovely carpet with yellow flowers .

The flower clusters of 'Autumn Joy' change color with the seasons.

A large carpet of 'Ruby Glow' becomes a brilliant blaze of color.

SOLIDAGO HYBRIDS

(sol-i-DAY-go)

Goldenrod

2'
1'

- Great summer to fall color
- Good cut or dried
- Easy and adaptable
- Zones 3–7

This native does *not* cause hayfever. **USES:** Combines wonderfully with all the daisy-type flowers, which bloom at same time, and especially well with aster or boltonia.

SITING AND CARE: Plant in full sun in well-drained soil. Space 18 inches apart. Water in dry weather. Division is seldom necessary.

Tassles of goldenrod 'Fireworks' reveal how this plant got its name.

RECOMMENDED VARIETIES: 'Fireworks' has yellow flowers with red-tinged foliage. 'Peter Pan' is bright yellow and stands 2 to 3 feet tall.

The compact plumes of 'Golden Baby' appear earlier, by midsummer.

Horizontal leaves of silver spike grass combine well with juniper and broom.

SPODIOPOGON SIBIRICUS

(spoh-dee-oh-POH-gon)

Silver spike grass

- Bold, dark green leaves
- Silvery flowers, summer to fall
- Red fall foliage
- Zones 4–8

Also known as frost grass, the foliage of silver spike grass becomes brown with streaks and tinges of deep purplish red in autumn. Erect clumps stand 5 feet tall in flower, blooming in late summer.

USES: Its fan-shaped form and long-lasting flowers make it perfect as a single specimen, planted in a group, or in masses. Looks wonderful with late-season perennials such as aster and stonecrop (Sedum 'Autumn Joy'). Or, place it in front of evergreens that will highlight its airy flowers. Flowers and foliage look lovely in cut arrangements.

SITING AND CARE: Plant in full sun or light shade. Will also grow in deeper shade but may require staking. Silver spike grass is not fussy about soil, but prefers it moist and well-drained. Best with regular watering or rainfall. Space 4 feet apart. Cut to the ground when foliage withers after frost.

STACHYS BYZANTINA

(STAY-kiss)

Lamb's-ear

Soft and wooly, silvery-white Stachys 'Big Ears' is fun to touch.

- Purplish pink flowers
- Outstanding foliage
- Easy and long-lived
- Zones 4–7

This low, tufted plant is prized for its 6- to 12-inch-tall, fuzzy-velvet foliage. It tends to rot, however, in damp, humid, climates.

USES: Irresistible to children, lamb's ear is also eye-catching at the front of a border. It coordinates with any color, but is especially useful to tone down hot colors, like black-eyed Susan (Rudbeckia) or butterfly milkweed (Asclepias), particularly on moonlit nights.

SITING AND CARE: Plant in full sun in well-drained, poor to average soil. Space 10 to 15 inches apart. Avoid overwatering. Divide every 4 years or as needed to rejuvenate clumps that begin to die out in the center. Gently rake out or hand pull winter-tattered leaves in spring to make room for new growth.

RECOMMENDED VARIETIES: 'Big Ears'/'Helen von Stein' has leaves 2 or 3 times as big; it performs well in hot climates. 'Silver Carpet' doesn't bloom, ideal for those who prefer a carpet of foliage. 'Cotton Boll' has unusual flowers consisting of fuzzy woolen clusters 12 inches tall. 'Primrose Heron' has foliage which emerges golden in spring and turns grey-green over the summer.

STIPA GIGANTEA

(STEE-pah)

Giant feather grass

Magnificent flowers on 5-foot stems rise from clumps of feather grass.

- Golden flowers
- Waves in the wind
- Drought tolerant
- Zones 7–10

The one-foot Mexican feather grass has silky "pony-tail" seed heads.

Sometimes called needle grass, the flowers of giant feather grass rise above clumps of 2-foot-tall foliage.

USES: The flowers of giant feather grass are fantastic, both in the garden and in bouquets. In warm areas, plant with late-blooming perennials such as aster, so they can fill the gap if the cool-season grass browns out in heat. Excellent in the mixed border.

SITING AND CARE: Plant in full sun in light, well-drained soil. Best as a specimen. Allow 3 feet between plants. Water regularly.

RELATED SPECIES: Mexican feather grass (S. tenuissima) has a more fluid look with silky June flowers. Heat tolerant to zone 7.

STOKESIA LAEVIS

(stoh-KEE-zee-uh)

Stokes' aster

18"

18"

- Weeks of blooms, summer to fall
- Wonderful for cutting
- Attracts butterflies
- Zone 5–9

Beautiful daisies of lavender, blue, or white bloom on 12-to 18-inch plants. This southern native is a fashionable, long-blooming garden subject, attractive to butterflies.
USES: Striking flowers with ragged petals and fuzzy centers are perfect for planting in drifts at the front of the informal border. Excellent cut flower. Goldenrod (*Solidago*) makes a worthy partner.
SITING AND CARE: Plant in full sun (or partial shade in southern regions) in well-drained soil. Sow seed outdoors in spring or space plants 12 to 15 inches apart. Removed faded flowers to extend bloom season. Divide every four years, or when clumps get crowded. Provide winter mulch in the North.
RECOMMENDED VARIETIES: 'Blue Danube' is a superb performer, with lavender-blue, 4-inch flowers. 'Blue Moon' has hyacinth blue flowers. 'Silver Moon' has creamy white flowers. 'Wyoming' is the deepest blue variety.

The showy flower of Stokes' aster looks like a big bachelor's button.

THALICTRUM ROCHEBRUNIANUM

(thah-LICK-trum)

Meadow rue

3'

2'

- Lavender late-spring flower
- Delicate, lacy leaves
- Tall, airy plants
- Zones 4–9

Foliage looks like a tall (3 to 6 feet) maidenhair fern; lavender flowers are a very pretty bonus.
USES: This meadow rue is a splendid background plant, able to rise 5 or 6 feet tall, but it looks better in groups of three.
SITING AND CARE: Plant in partial shade in deep, rich, moist soil high in organic matter. Space 24 inches apart. Water in dry weather. Divide every five years or as necessary to relieve crowding.
RECOMMENDED VARIETIES AND RELATED SPECIES: 'Lavender Mist' boasts purple stems and frosted yellow and deep lavender flowers. Columbine meadow rue (*T. aquilegiifolium*) is shorter, with foliage resembling columbine, and with dense flower heads in bright colors. A white variety ('Album') exists. Double meadow rue (*T. delavayi* 'Hewitt's Double') is 3 to 5 feet tall, with clouds of tiny double lilac flowers. Kyoshu meadow rue (*T. kiusianum*) is only 4 to 6 inches tall with delicate, gray-green foliage tinted purple; the foliage is more showy than its tiny lavender flowers.

Columbine meadow rue bears dense flower heads in shades of pink.

TIARELLA CORDIFOLIA

(tee-uh-REL-uh)

Allegheny foam flower

12"

18"

- Spring flowers
- Handsome foliage
- Bronzy-red fall color
- Zones 3–8

Spikes of starry flowers rise above 6- to 8-inch-tall, maple-like foliage. Leaves can turn red, yellow in fall.
USES: Allegheny foam flower spreads by stolons, making a great ground cover for woodland gardens, and is especially pretty when paired with bleeding heart (*Dicentra*).
SITING AND CARE: Plant in shade in moist, humus-rich, well-drained soil. Space 12 to 15 inches apart. Can be thinned when plants become crowded.
RECOMMENDED VARIETIES AND RELATED SPECIES: A great deal of effort has gone into improving this species. 'Dark Eyes', for example, has pale pink flowers arising from leaves splashed heavily with inky black, that turn an interesting bronze in winter. Wherry's foam flower (*T. wherryi*) is similar to T. cordifolia, with showy flower spikes on 10-inch-tall, evergreen plants. It doesn't spread by stolons.

The airy clusters of creamy-white Allegheny foam flower seem to float.

Exquisite 'Miyazaki' toad lily blooms
resemble miniature orchids.

TRICYRTIS HIRTA

(try-SIR-tiss)

Toad lily

30"

18"

- ■ Autumn flowers
- ■ Great for cutting
- ■ Easy and reliable
- ■ Zones 4–8 (zone 7, east of the Rocky Mountains

Graceful, arching stems with shingle-like leaves grow 20 to 30 inches tall. Within its range it does well in all but desert climates.
USES: This is one of the more interesting flowers for the shady garden, particularly for fall. Put near the path, so you can view the blossoms at close range.
SITING AND CARE: Plant in filtered light or medium shade in humus-rich, acid, moist, well-drained soil. Space 12 to 18 inches apart. Mulch with pine needles or shredded oak leaves.
RECOMMENDED VARIETIES AND RELATED SPECIES: 'Miyazaki' has white flowers with lilac spots. 'Tojen' has large, white flowers tinged with lavender-purple. 'White Towers' is a shorter form, 18 to 20 inches tall, with pure white flowers. *T. formosana* 'Amethystina' has lavender-blue flowers with creamy throats and red spots, in bloom from late July until frost.

White flowers with red "eyes" on
the majestic stalks of Verbascum
chaixii

VERBASCUM CHAIXII

(ver-BASS-kum)

Mullein

3'

2'

- ■ Blooms all summer
- ■ Wooly, gray-green foliage
- ■ Drought tolerant
- ■ Zones 5–8

Flower stalks shoot up from a broad rosette of leaves in early summer. Usually short-lived but will thrive and self-sow in dry climates.
USES: Its 30-inch spires provide a strong vertical accent.
SITING AND CARE: Plant in full sun or partial shade in light, well-drained, alkaline soil. Space 18 inches apart. Cut back flower stalk after blooming to encourage side branches, which will bloom later.
RECOMMENDED VARIETIES AND RELATED SPECIES: 'Album' has white flowers with purple centers. 'Silver Candelabra' grows to 5 feet, with branched flower stems and wooly, silver foliage. *V. × phoeniceum* 'Cotswold Queen' has pinkish bronze flowers, with lilac centers. 'Mont Blanc' is a pure white version. *V. olympicum*, Olympic mullein, forms a mound of wooly whitish gray leaves from which emerges a 3- to 6-foot tall stalk with branches of golden yellow flowers. Zones 6 to 8.

Verbena canadensis *blooms all*
summer with bright flower clusters.

VERBENA HYBRIDS

(ver-BEE-na)

Creeping verbena

1'

3'

- ■ All-summer colorful ground cover
- ■ Good for cutting
- ■ Attracts butterflies
- ■ Zones 6–10 (annual in the North)

Glossy green, foot-tall mat spreads out 3 feet or more.
USES: An easy plant for all-season blooms, verbena looks great cascading over a rock wall, or in the rock garden paired with pinks (*Dianthus*). Suitable for edging or for growing in containers, including hanging baskets.
SITING AND CARE: Plant in full sun; moist, well-drained soil is essential. Space plants 18 inches apart. Prone to aphids, whiteflies, slugs, snails, and spider mites.
RECOMMENDED VARIETIES AND RELATED SPECIES: 'Homestead Purple' has large, velvety purple blossoms. 'Sissinghurst' is bright pink with lacy foliage. Tall verbena (*V. bonariensis*) bears 3- to 4-foot-tall wiry, branching stems with heads of tiny purple-blue flowers that bloom summer to fall. Hardy in zones 7 to 10, but reseeds delightfully for year-to-year effect in colder zones.

VERONICA HYBRIDS

(vuh-RON-ih-ka)

Speedwell

24"
18"
- Rich blues, summer to fall
- Good for cutting
- Long-lived
- Zones 3–8

Members of this large group of plants grow 1 to 3 feet tall.
USES: Veronica is excellent in the middle of the border, in a clump as a specimen plant, or in the rock garden. It is beautiful with yellow varieties of daylilies (*Hemerocallis*).
SITING AND CARE: Plant in full sun in poor to average, well-drained soil. Space 12 to 18 inches apart. Remove spent blossoms to prolong

Veronica spicata incana boasts spikes of blue and silvery foliage.

blooming. Divide every four years.
RECOMMENDED VARIETIES AND RELATED SPECIES: *V. alpina* 'Goodness Grows', 12 inches tall, is a long-blooming blue. *V. peduncularis* 'Georgia Blue' has blue flowers on 12-inch mats of purple-backed foliage. *V. spicata* 'Red Fox' has glossy leaves and 15-inch spikes of red flowers. 'Sunny Border Blue' is 18 to 24 inches tall with dark blue flowers.

Veronica 'Georgia Blue' forms six-inch mats of blue.

VIOLA ODORATA

(VYE-oh-luh)

Sweet violet

8"
12"
- Exquisite spring fragrance
- Violet, rose, or white
- Good for cutting
- Zones 6–8 (zone 7, east of the Rocky Mountains)

This is the sweet-smelling violet of literature. Six- to 8-inch plants spread a foot or more wide.
USES: Unsurpassed for fragrance, sweet violet is wonderful for naturalizing in the woodland garden or for bordering a path.

SITING AND CARE: Plant in partial shade in moist, humus-rich soil. Sow seeds in fall or space plants a foot apart in spring.
RECOMMENDED VARIETIES AND RELATED SPECIES: 'Rosina' is a long-blooming pink. 'Royal Robe'

A patch of blue: violet 'Jewel Blue' shows off the yellow center and dark netted markings in the throat.

has vibrant purple flowers. *V. cornuta* 'Arkwright Ruby' has 1-inch, dark-eyed maroon flowers. Reblooms if deadheaded. Zones 6 to 9. Bird's-foot violet (*V. pedata*) is one of the prettiest natives and looks just like its name. Hardy in zones 4 to 8.

Sweet violet's fragrant blossoms and its heart-shaped leaves have made it a favorite flower for centuries.

YUCCA FILAMENTOSA

(YUH-ka)

Yucca

6'
3'
- Fragrant, creamy white summer bells
- Great spiky foliage
- Evergreen foliage
- Zones 4–10

Huge flower stems rises 3 to 12 feet above knee-high foliage.
USES: Yucca brings a romantic Southwest accent to the garden.
SITING AND CARE: Plant in full sun in sandy, well-drained soil. Space 3 feet apart. Remove spent flowers and tattered older leaves for

better appearance. Drought tolerant.
RECOMMENDED VARIETIES AND RELATED SPECIES: 'Variegata' has green-and-yellow-

Yucca's magnificent flower stalks are unforgettable and last for weeks.

striped leaves. 'Bright Edge' bears leaves with yellow edges. *Y. filifera* has small leaves. Soapweed (*Y. glauca*) is the hardiest yucca (zones 3–10).

Yucca filamentosa 'Golden Sword' provides an architectural form and dramatic flair to the home landscape.

THE USDA PLANT HARDINESS ZONE MAP OF NORTH AMERICA

Plants are classified according to the amount of cold weather they can handle. For example, a plant listed as hardy to zone 6 will survive a winter in which the temperature drops to minus 10° F.

Warm weather also influences whether a plant will survive in your region. Although this map does not address heat hardiness, in general, if a range of hardiness zones are listed for a plant, the plant will survive winter in the coldest zone as well as tolerate the heat of the warmest zone.

To use this map, find the approximate location of your community, then match the color band marking that area to the zone key at left.

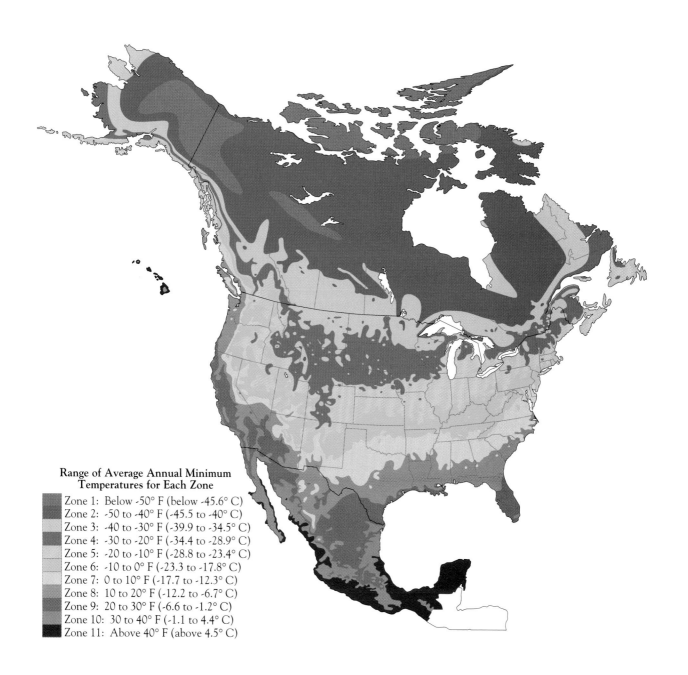

Range of Average Annual Minimum Temperatures for Each Zone

Zone 1: Below -50° F (below -45.6° C)
Zone 2: -50 to -40° F (-45.5 to -40° C)
Zone 3: -40 to -30° F (-39.9 to -34.5° C)
Zone 4: -30 to -20° F (-34.4 to -28.9° C)
Zone 5: -20 to -10° F (-28.8 to -23.4° C)
Zone 6: -10 to 0° F (-23.3 to -17.8° C)
Zone 7: 0 to 10° F (-17.7 to -12.3° C)
Zone 8: 10 to 20° F (-12.2 to -6.7° C)
Zone 9: 20 to 30° F (-6.6 to -1.2° C)
Zone 10: 30 to 40° F (-1.1 to 4.4° C)
Zone 11: Above 40° F (above 4.5° C)

INDEX

Pages numbers followed by t indicate material in tables. Numbers in italics denote photographs. Boldface numbers refer to lead entries in the "Selection and Growing Guide."

METRIC CONVERSIONS

U.S. Units to Metric Equivalents			Metric Units to U.S. Equivalents		
To Convert From	Multiply By	To Get	To Convert From	Multiply By	To Get
Inches	25.4	Millimeters	Millimeters	0.0394	Inches
Inches	2.54	Centimeters	Centimeters	0.3937	Inches
Feet	30.48	Centimeters	Centimeters	0.0328	Feet
Feet	0.3048	Meters	Meters	3.2808	Feet
Yards	0.9144	Meters	Meters	1.0936	Yards
Square inches	6.4516	Square centimeters	Square centimeters	0.1550	Square inches
Square feet	0.0929	Square meters	Square meters	10.764	Square feet
Square yards	0.8361	Square meters	Square meters	1.1960	Square yards
Acres	0.4047	Hectares	Hectares	2.4711	Acres
Cubic inches	16.387	Cubic centimeters	Cubic centimeters	0.0610	Cubic inches
Cubic feet	0.0283	Cubic meters	Cubic meters	35.315	Cubic feet
Cubic feet	28.316	Liters	Liters	0.0353	Cubic feet
Cubic yards	0.7646	Cubic meters	Cubic meters	1.308	Cubic yards
Cubic yards	764.55	Liters	Liters	0.0013	Cubic yards

To convert from degrees Fahrenheit (F) to degrees Celsius (C), first subtract 32, then multiply by ⅝.

To convert from degrees Celsius to degrees Fahrenheit, multiply by ⅖, then add 32.